New Earth
The light be[yond]

By Sharon Milne Barbour

New Earth -
The light beyond the horizon

Copyright © 2020 by Sharon Milne Barbour - Bengalrose Healing
Published by Bengalrose Healing
Designed by Sharon Milne Barbour
Author - Sharon Milne Barbour
Book cover illustration – by CIMBart
Editors – Author and Di Reed

All rights are reserved. No part of this book may be reproduced by any mechanical, photographic, or electrical process, or in the form of a phonographic recording, nor may it be stored in a retrieval system, transmitted, or otherwise be copied for public or private use - other than for "fair use" as brief quotations embodied in articles. The verses can be read to private or public audience. Reviews not to be written without prior written knowledge of the publisher and author. The intent of the author is only to offer information of a general nature to help you on your spiritual path. In the event you use any of the information in the book for yourself, which is your right, the author and the publisher assumes no responsibility for your actions.

We are all responsible for our own life journeys and are caretakers of the spaces we live in...

When a civilisation struggles to reach its full potential because its people cannot work in unity, it will eventually self-destruct, taking the life force space of the people with it.

Many millennia of humanity's history lie wasted and forgotten in the layers of Earth's dust. Many times over this planet's history, civilisation has been rebuilt in the hope humanity can live as one. Always, there is the continued hope that a new world will emerge and exist in the continuous light energy of love and not the darkness of hate and fear.

Earth's story is told across many of the universe's civilisations, used as a teaching example for others to learn from. It brings to them the lesson that if you do not listen to your life force space and respect your own kind, the utopia that is often sought is never found.

We now bring to you the story of a brave new world. A world where through struggle, hardship, passion and love, a utopia emerged from the dust of lost ancient times.

Life journal

Home planet Diacurat

Life journal section –
'New Earth - The light beyond the horizon'

Transmissions begin…

Life Journal – transmission 1
New Earth - The light beyond the horizon

Welcome to this section of my life journal, 'The light beyond the horizon'. For your understanding this is a translation into your language and current time frame matrix. My main life journal is a mind communication transmission recording of what I choose to relay about my life. At the end of my life it becomes available from the universal knowledge library for all to tap into and learn from my life's journey, to help guide future generations.

Only the chosen beings selected by the Intergalactic Council can access this special section of my journal. When you connect to it, the words of my language will be translated to all your levels of understanding, based on the dimensional existence you inhabit. Higher ascended capability beings with thought mind control will be able to download this section of my journal to their minds and technology for future knowledge purposes; for others, it is available in their printed written language.

The reason for starting a separate journal section for this next phase of my life is that I have chosen to be part of my planet's incarnation program. As with all Diacuratians who enter the program we keep a separate section in our life's journal that records this event. These transmissions will go into our learning libraries of the universal knowledge library. I know that whatever the outcome of this new adventure, it will bring great knowledge after my physical life phase has ended on my home planet.

Now I had better introduce myself, as the off-world beings

reading this section of my journal will not know whom I am! You are reading this part of the life journal by Anikelican, or my shortened affectionate name is Anike. My home planet is Diacurat, based in a galaxy in the fourth galactic quadrant in the Coma Berenices, within the prime universe of Delta. Our planet lies on one of the outer spirals with our light star. We have three moons and seven other planets also revolve round our light star, but only ours has intelligent life forms. I will have great pleasure in describing my home planet through these transmissions, so please be patient with me as my story unfolds.

As I record this transmission, I am sitting in the learning school of meditation and multidimensional travel, which is named after its founder member Touliza. Touliza was the first of our kind to join the incarnation program on the planet Earth 11722 years ago of their Earth time. They chose the time of the last Atlantis experiment program that ran on Earth. We have also chosen Earth for my incarnation, in the twenty-third century year of 2222.

I think it is best if I explain the time frame of Earth life in relation to time on Diacurat, and how this affects an incarnated multidimensional being's view of their Earth incarnation existence. The length of our light days varies between the two planets and we are in a different reality and dimension. Every one of our light days is seven Earth months in the understanding of time dimensional light frequency differences. In Touliza's time frame we could scroll back and forth to view an incarnated existence up to the point where the Earth time coincides with mine. Now, we can also jump forward on the time line to see the path the humanoid physical body will take based on their existence and the decisions taken so far on their time line.

I have been inspired in my education by this famous Diacuratian Touliza, who led the way for this amazing program and the changes it brought to our planet, over 1674 hyons of our timeline ago.

The program is still overseen by the Diacurat Sacred Light Council and the Intergalactic Council, but so much has altered since those first steps were taken.

For example, in Touliza's time frame we relied a lot on other off-world civilisation friends to help us with the multidimensional travel and the incarnation process. The beings that helped us were from Lemurian, Pleiadian, Andromeda, Arcturian and Salcariton, also part of the Intergalactic Council. We are now self-sufficient at this process and are also teachers to other civilisations that are stepping into the incarnation program for the first time. It would be worth you reading Touliza's transcripts under the section 'The light within Atlantis' as it will enlighten you about the history and the pioneering steps of the incarnation program. This can be found in the universal knowledge library or as a book if you exist in a three-dimensional plane.

Life Journal – transmission 2
New Earth - The light beyond the horizon

I live in the main city of Diacurat, called Corthion with my life-bonded partner Baltrexn. We have been bonded together for ten hyons now and I will tell you more about us I'm sure, but here is a quick summary for you, so you understand my life journey so far.

I am a historian of my people and I have the pleasure to study our own history as well as the history of many off-world civilisations. The planets and dimensions I study are all under the umbrella of the Intergalactic Council. There are thousands of them, and while I mainly specialise in, Castrolian, Planet Xerioc One, Cardigon and Zelcriton, I am always looking for that new historical adventure to follow.

My partner Baltrexn is a star ship medical officer. He is a specialist in the anatomy of many species so he can give healing; he also has access to the universal knowledge of all species and their physical biological or ethereal requirements. He is on one of the intergalactic star ship vessels that travel the universe on behalf of the overseers, who preside over mediation and guidance with species to help with the ascension process and joining the Intergalactic Council. He also gives training on our off-world medical station above our planet. His work sometimes takes him away for long periods, but we stay close in mind link and by technology – we are nearly always mind linked when not physically together.

We met when we were young students at the learning school of meditation and multidimensional travel, which is now part of all Diacuratian education. The young of our world are taught meditation from a very young age which then leads to the journey of creating the multidimensional ethereal self. At the point of maturity these merge, and we then learn to create the inner power to leave our planet and undertake multidimensional travel.

I am an only child; my parents are mother Delikan and father Philion. My mother is a very creative individual and is a creator and designer of garments. She also now teaches, using her knowledge to help and guide others to bring more creativity to our garments for all occasions. My father is an ambassador and is part of the Sacred Light Council. He oversees high level events associated with off-world visits. Of course, I also have more extended family and friends but really, they are not part of this incarnation journey I am about to embark on. To complete my and Baltrexn's family is our pet Peagal, a wonderful creature who I can best describe as a flying bird/lizard. He has the ability to camouflage himself, which can lead to times when we cannot find him, but when I have his favourite treat, he soon emerges from his hiding spot. He is a very intelligent and affectionate creature originating from the planet Cardigon, which has a similar atmosphere as ours.

I have mentioned the Sacred Light Council, which is one of two councils that oversee our planet; the other is the off-world Intergalactic Council. The Sacred Light Council is made up of Diacuratian ascended light masters, ambassadors, light priests and priestesses. They all have the power to project their minds across great distances, linking with their own kind and other species in the universe. These Diacuratians have given over their lives to this purpose to make sure we stay in the pure love energy space we now inhabit, living for the one and the good of all. They meditate for long periods every light day, focusing on the pure energy of the planet and the energy of the universe. With each generation their consciousness energy and knowledge has grown and is passed on to all Diacuratians. All Diacuratians choose to strive for this ascension and we now have all achieved full ethereal ascension. We still use the physical body but can now choose to have ethereal multidimensional bodies with pure conscious energy. As I said, Touliza was one of the pioneers of this amazing leap for our planet; it took another three generations to achieve this. I think the consensus of opinion among our citizens is we wish to have the choice to hold onto the physical body, using the multidimensional split as a way to travel the universe. The biggest breakthrough that took us to the next level of ascension was the ability to create an ethereal body for multidimensional travel and rematerialise into our physical form through manipulation of the energy frequency of molecules and light energy source. This is done through mind control and tuning into the light frequencies of our own physical structure and the space around us. We can also create spaceships that can be multidimensional for travelling long distances with living ethereal multidimensional life forms. When the ship and species reach its destination, it transforms back to its physical forms and structures.

The overseers created the Intergalactic Council. They are from a divine source of pure bliss, unconditional love and light in the tenth to twelfth dimension energy realms of universe Delta. They are energy beings beyond anything you could ever imagine. They have energy form with vast consciousness and a hierarchy of ascension within their own existence. Compared to Diacurat, with our more limited vision and energy existence, their reality is beyond anything you will ever see here. To the lower third dimension energy planets in the universe, where this divine source has chosen to touch them with their light, they can be seen as gods. If we look at our own planet's history, we find that we thought the same a long time ago. But now we understand them more, and see that they do not want to be worshipped, just listened to, so they can be a guiding light for all beings.

On Diacurat many thousands of hyons ago, we were lower energy beings, existing in a lower energy state of mind and body. Over hyons, we started to realise that if we did not connect to our planet and its life source we would perish through self-destruction. We did not have highly ascended incarnated souls to help us with this; we came to this understanding because the overseers chose to visit us and give us our life light crystal. As you can imagine, this was a time of great change for our planet. At first, there were ones among us who feared the beings of light and love, but time soon healed that fear and helped us progress into the light energy.

The overseers created the Intergalactic Council for the purpose of bringing all ascended beings they had helped and guided together as one. The council oversees the contact of new species, guiding all species to work together in unity, creating alliances and guiding those selected along the ascension path of light. Each species that is at this level of consciousness selects members of their own high council to sit on the Intergalactic Council. This council then supports the work of the overseers through the universe Delta and beyond.

Life Journal – transmission 3
New Earth - The light beyond the horizon

I am pleased to say I can finally put up my feet and rest this light day. Well, resting to me means catching up on my transmissions, linking with Baltrexn on his ship and watching the fading light star and the moons merging while they dance as reflections on the lake. While watching this beauty I listen to the day creatures fall silent and the night creatures slowly find their tune for the night's chorus of beautiful song. This is one of my favourite times of our light day as it starts to fade to dark; I always find peace and tune into myself for self-reflection and healing at this time.

My light day was especially busy as I met my incarnation team for the first time at the mind and body travel institute. The mind and body travel institute is the facility on our planet that oversees all the multidimensional travel and energy body splits such as reflection of self-body splits for incarnation and mind merges. It also links to a space station above our planet and has a light portal that takes the travellers to their destinations. I had already met Havrium who runs the incarnation program. The other Diacurat members are Uculium, a multidimensional split specialist, Ourriyn, who observes and monitors the higher self, me, and the incarnated soul self. Pecion ensures all that takes place is recorded and tagged with correct access for those who need the information. We also have Ionkul from the Salcariton race, who have been part of the Earth incarnation program from the late Atlantis times. Actually, they really helped the overseers with this process and their knowledge and technology aided great advancements in the program. I must not forget Freylen from the Pleiadian race; she is going to be my support through this incarnation journey, my mentor and study companion. Freylen has also incarnated on to Earth, which was in a timeline called the Egyptian period. This is a fascinating culture that links with the greater universe, and I will enlighten you on another transmission about my Egyptian study highlights.

The meeting was mainly to discuss the process that will lead up to the incarnation. My first task is to study pivotal times in the Earth's history; this knowledge will help with my human bond and self-understanding of the time frame I am to enter. This is because the history of a civilisation leads to future events; it helps me to understand the thought processes behind decisions made by the humans and overseers. Havrium gave me a list to follow for studying, so I will get on to this task soon. I just love absorbing knowledge and studying history, and I can see from the list that I have already studied some of them, so that cuts back my time frame on this a little bit.

When this study period is complete, I will then learn about the time frame on Earth I will be entering, and my life's guided path. Part of this will be gathering with other beings beforehand who will be part of this incarnation experience. I am so excited as I relay these thoughts to you, as I cannot wait to start this journey.

Life Journal – transmission 4
New Earth - The light beyond the horizon

I rose early this light day to make a start on my study of Earth's history. I am going to do most of it from my living space, as this is where I normally work, unless I go to visit a history site of interest on our world or another planet. I also sometimes work at the Kihackin History Institute, sharing my studies with other masters and students. My study area looks out across the lake in front of my living space, which is a great energy space for mind enhancing. I also find the floribunda beautiful to observe and the scents that fill the air. There is one particular flower that is large and purple in colour, in the light day it shimmers in the light and looks as if it reflects the world around. It closes in the dark, resting and waiting for the next light day to show us its beauty again.

My main study this light day will be the Earth that has existed over 4.5 billion Earth years ago, with its early molten rock state cooling to a living planet that could sustain life. As a young planet, Earth faced an early impact by a rogue planet, which caused a break off of mineral materials that then formed its moon. Its position from the light star being an advantage, the three heavenly bodies of Earth, Moon and Sun could then work together to create the Earth we know as the Blue Planet.

As the Earth cooled and formed, micro-organisms were created, which were the basis of its original life forms. Creating its atmosphere for the life of plants and animals and creating a gravity that would sustain life-giving water for the planet, it then evolved over millions of years.

The development of this blue jewel planet was watched from

afar by the overseers and other civilisations across the universe. Earth was attractive to other species which perhaps would benefit from mining the minerals it had to offer, or as a base for travelling across the universe and exploring its galaxies. Over millions of years Earth has had off-world visitors, some as science observers, some building a base for future colonisation and others for mining minerals.

The nearby planet Mars was also once a blue planet but sadly, due to a planet-wide eco disaster it was laid waste to a barren state and its atmosphere was lost. Mars and other planets in the Earth's solar system have been used for colonisation, with space stations for portal travel. Many of these species have stayed cloaked from the human eye, only to reveal themselves when the time is right.

As my mind scrolls the early Earth records, I can see all of the history of these early pioneers. For various reasons, some of these early colonists left the planet or chose to stay, not returning to their home planet. This is the start of the Earth's humanoid species' existence. Looking forward in the planet's history many great human minds thought the human race evolved from the monkey primates co-existing there, or from Adam and Eve, created by a God that created humans. But there is no mystery for humanity; the human species that exists on Earth in the modern time frame comes from a mix of occupation and experiments over a couple of million years. For modern humanity there is no evidence of this to the visible eye, as over time the Earth reclaims structures created in previous eras. If I took you to the Earth in the twenty-first century, and humanity left the planet, it would take up to a thousand Earth years to reclaim the structures of humanity. Some would have perished into the soil. Others would be hidden under hills and mountains or under the risen seas. Some can be preserved, and as a historian, this is what I love to rediscover – and help planets rediscover – their history.

During these transmissions I will reveal to you the key points of some of these, to help you understand Earth's history timeline.

Life Journal – transmission 5
New Earth - The light beyond the horizon

I have just returned from watching my mother's garment show. She is a master of her craft and teaches at the Pekenion Centre for the arts. Once a hyon, her students put on a show of their designs and creativity. This includes garments and jewellery. As a species we take great pride in our appearance and our garments reflect individual occupations and personalities.

My mother makes my garments. Some are for work and these are hard-wearing, as a lot of the time when I am on historical sites, I get dirty and need something that's tough and self-cleans quickly. Then I like the lighter, softer materials for my comfortable day wear when I am studying or relaxing.

So as I set up for my study period, I am wearing my comfortable all-in-one garment, designed by my mother in a calming green – I find this colour relaxes me, and helps me focus. Colours have energy, frequencies and vibration and they react with our minds and physical makeup.

Freylen is going to join me on my studies, as she also needs to study to update herself on Earth's history and tell me of her experiences with her incarnation there. It is important we have a close relationship, as she is my mentor beforehand, and hopes to be a guide during my incarnation. She has a lovely energy and such a calm, clear clarity in her thinking and perception of everything. Freylen has a more scientific mind than mine and we feel this will be a good balance; her logical thinking and my passion for history will help balance my perception of the events I reveal to you.

We will gain our knowledge from the universal knowledge

library where all is recorded and stored by the overseers and Intergalactic Council. We connect by energy light and harmonic sound frequency settings, which is provided to those with permission to access to this knowledge. We are only given access to the areas we need; this is so we stay focused on the task in hand. This is especially good for me, as my history-curious mind would want to explore the pasts of many civilisations, but this is for my future study, not for now. We link our minds to the frequencies given us, then through what you would understand as a vision that we see in our minds, we link to the knowledge we require. With our minds we can then guide ourselves through the information, gathering what we need. In the time of Touliza they used a combination of crystal screens and mind-to-mind connection. We have now advanced way beyond using technology of this sort, which is very exciting for our ascension. Also, Freylen can link her mind with the library and mine and we can work together studying and discussing what we have learnt, either in our minds or with verbal communication.

We have decided to start with the earlier occupants of ascension beings on Earth over two billion years of Earth's time. This was a time before the overseers created the Intergalactic Council. The attraction of Earth to beings in the universe was as a young planet for any mineral ores it would develop. It was starting to cool down; there were large oceans and it was still forming its landmasses. The first species to land on Earth was the Delarafons, best described as a race of physical beings of humanoid appearance. In one way, they were a very intelligent, mixed gender race. They were tall with thick hide skins and large heads with flat ears, small yellow eyes and flat noses. They had no body hair and an odour you would describe as an acid smell. They had a very simple spoken language and mind-to-mind control as well. They wore what's best described as bio armour body suits that protected them from the heat of Earth's hottest volcanic areas. They came from a planet of high volcanic activity which they had mined dry. With their space technology they could travel through the light frequencies of time, harmonic sound and colour to selected destinations. Unfortunately, their intelligence did not allow them the foresight of the harm they were doing to their own planet and existence.

They existed in a toxic atmosphere that would be harmful to modern Earth humans. But back in their time period they discovered Earth, that it was also of high volcanic activity with a toxic atmosphere as the planet formed, and this was its attraction. They surveyed the layers of the Earth's crust and one area contained the mineral they were seeking. They mined it to the point that none was left, so they left with it; as a result, they changed the fabric of the planet's materialisation process and how she would develop. This was a time when the planets were not being watched all the time by the overseers; if they had been, they would not have allowed another race to desecrate a planet's natural resource. The Delarafons no longer exist; their planet eventually died after they had died out, as it could no longer sustain life. But they are remembered in the overseers recorded history of Earth as the first pioneers to visit the planet.

For our next study time period, there was a big gap then in human understanding of time, which covered 440 million Earth years. By this time, Earth had developed its oxygen atmosphere, first plants, reptiles, fish and amphibious species. It had taken millions of years for the planet to get to this stage. It developed a pure, clear atmosphere and was quite moist in places with long periods of rain creating lush green areas on the lands. This is when Earth's high energy frequency started to shine out into the universe; her energy vibration was now strong and noticeable to other ascension societies and the overseers in the universe. Earth was added to the overseers' portfolio of planets to explore, with the hope it would one day sustain intelligent life or be a candidate for experiments with new life. The most well-known of these was the Atlantis experiments that lasted over 300,000 Earth years, but I now must divert back to 440 million years ago.

The next race to arrive on earth was the Pelcarians. Freylen is quite excited by this, as they were scientific explorers for their kind. The Pelcarians were from a planet similar to Earth, although it is six times its size, with a thinner atmosphere. They were a beautiful and graceful race of beings, with mixed gender. They were tall and slim with delicate features, silvery blond hair, highly intelligent and peaceful. They only ever sought knowledge and the records show they were excited by the history of Earth's evolution.

They built a large biosphere city with its own self-contained atmosphere as a base. Then they used their spacecrafts and land vehicles to explore the planet, collecting rock samples through mining, as well as plants and creatures for their data. Freylen was excited when she looked at modern Earth's history, as a piece of evidence of this time had been found. Humans had named it the 'The London Hammer', because it was found in an area called London, Texas. The Pelcarians used simple hand tools for breaking open rock samples. She saw this had confused humanity, with some saying something so old must have travelled back through time. In fact, it had been preserved in rock over 400 million years old. Their minds could not understand that it belonged to an early occupant of Earth, and was used for small mining exploration.

Another thing for you to consider is that when an alien race lands on a new planet, it could be susceptible to new disease and also leave behind, say, new bacteria that Earth had not yet developed. This race was very conscious of this and took precautions not to leave a heavy footprint of their existence on Earth. They stayed connected to the planet for over a thousand Earth years, with a scientific community based on the planet. They also used this base to explore the Earth's solar system to gather knowledge to help sustain their own existence.

Their home planet still exists but sadly, due to an unforeseen disease that spread through their civilisations, they perished. It was believed to have been brought back to their planet from one of their many science ships, the disease ravaging their physical bodies. Even with all their knowledge they could not prevent it. They kept some ships away and they found new homes, but sadly there is no record now of any survivors as I record this knowledge to you.

Freylen has just learned that Pelcarians' planet has also had lots of visits from other off-world civilisations but none as yet have chosen to settle there. The reason for this is that there is a natural primitive species developing into an intelligent species again on the planet. So for now, the overseers wish to let them progress without interference. Of course, science has moved on and we get treated for any possible disease we might contract from other species, and this allows for safe exploration of the universe. There is always precaution, but there have been no cases recorded like this for many, many hyons now. I myself visit many other planets to study their history and have been fine, we are always checked on our return to the science space station before we continue our journey to our destination on the planet.

It might also be interesting for you to know that Freylen comes from a different atmosphere to our planet, but through her ascension she can retune her body to adapt to our atmosphere and gravity for long periods of time. This is all made possible through light and sound frequencies. She carries her own regenerating capsule in her sleeping chambers, which ensures all her body cells are adjusted as needed, to keep her alive on our planet.

Life Journal – transmission 6
New Earth - The light beyond the horizon

We are looking forward to another light day studying Earth's history, but we both thought we would start the light day with a swim in the lake near my dwelling and then have breakfast. I enjoy the fruits of our world that are created in various ways of deliciousness for our palette. Freylen also enjoyed the breakfast and she told me some of the fruits' flavours are similar to those of her own world. We have technology that creates the dishes we require from mind activation. Many hyons ago we prepared our food by hand, but our ascension has allowed us to advance to this new way of processing our food. By breaking down the molecular structure frequencies, it is reprogrammed to create the dishes we decide to eat.

Feeling refreshed and focused we carried on our studies exploring the next occupants of Earth's history. The planet continued to be monitored by many of the universe's species, which are too many to be named, some perishing in the long time frame of Earth's history. I also understood these time frames could be hard to comprehend, as there are such large gaps. You need to understand that for an alien species to consider Earth as a colony to live on or as a candidate for scientific or mining exploration, there has to be some compatibility with the Earth and its atmosphere. Over millions of years the planet kept altering its atmosphere, which influenced the decisions of alien species on whether or not to consider it worth their while.

The next recorded race to make a home on Earth was 65 million years ago in Earth's time. The Karzarians were from a dying planet in the Milky Way Galaxy. They were a humanoid race similar to Pleiadians but not ascended from them. They were very fine featured and small in size, with white blond hair and piercing blue eyes that looked like cut crystal. They had mixed gender with the females being a bit larger than the males. The females were dominant in their civilisation and were often the leaders. They all had various occupations but lived in harmony – even more so after they lost their home planet, when they realised how precious life was.

They saw Earth as a future home as it had developed to a sustainable level by this time, giving hope for the future of their race. Their own planet was slowly fading with the light star that sustained their existence slowly dying. They were not multidimensional beings yet, and even though their science and technology were very advanced, they were not enough to save their sun and planet. They sent spaceships out into the Galaxy and beyond seeking a planet to sustain them. They found two – Earth, and one in the Andromeda galaxy. They connected with the Andromedan race, who understood their plight and helped them find a suitable planet. With their support, the Karzarians began the journey to their two new homes, Earth and Mikaydon.

These two planets provided a similar atmosphere that suited them, so they started their migration across the stars building new cities and communities. The successful migration to both planets was achieved in time before their light star became a super nova, taking its solar system with it. The Andromedans helped them with technology so the two planets stayed in contact every light day through light portals. For 90,000 Earth years they lived on Earth alongside the animal species, as well as introducing their own. They protected their cities and agricultural lands with a forcefield for protection against the larger, wilder Earth mammals, and the animals learnt to stay away, leaving them to live in harmony.

Then devastatingly, an asteroid came into Earth's solar system, and by the time it was discovered it was on course for the planet; as a peaceful race they had no weapons, and nor did the Andromedans. They soon realised it would cause a mass extinction event and had a few Earth days to evacuate to Mikaydon. Unfortunately, not all could be saved in the time they had; they then evacuated the remaining Karzarians to the part of the planet that would be spared from the projected impact, hoping to save them, but that part of Earth was no longer inhabitable and many Karzarians were lost; although a few were rescued, that was the end of their time on Earth.

This has been recorded in Earth's history by modern humanity as the Cretaceous Period extinction event, as a sudden mass extinction of some three-quarters of the plant and animal species, some of which had lived on Earth for over 165 million years. Earth then went into its next phase, which was recovery from the asteroid's impact. Earth was left alone for 30 million years to reset herself and regenerate with the animal and plant species left on the planet.

We are pleased to say Karzarians continued to thrive on their other chosen planet Mikaydon with the help of their Andromedan friends. They are now a highly ascended race, capable of physical multidimensional explorations and part of the Intergalactic Council.

Life Journal – transmission 7
New Earth - The light beyond the horizon

We have been working so hard these last few light days that we've decided to take a break tomorrow. But before we do that here is some more information for you to digest. The next recorded race to make a home on Earth was the Aorgturians, a humanoid race.

I think I should explain here what I mean by a humanoid race. A physically existing DNA cell race of single head, neck, four limbs, standing upright and with intelligence. They have eyes, ears, nose and mouth and some are telepathic of mind. They have to consume food and liquid to sustain themselves and can be of single or mixed gender. The name humanoid has been given to these types of beings for a long time; they have helped populate the planet Earth through their physical kind being left on the planet, and their DNA used to enhance Earth humans. Jumping to modern humans on Earth, as you read this in your timeline, many ascension species have contributed to the existing human DNA makeup.

Although the Earth was observed by many ascension species, it was not until three million years ago in the planet's history that it was occupied again. The Aorgturians chose Earth's moon as an outpost in the solar system and occupied a small area of planet Earth. They came from a galaxy which Earth humans now call Messier Eighty-Two; it is a starburst galaxy approximately twelve million Earth light-years away in the constellation Ursa Major. Their planet has a single star with 12 planets orbiting it, including some which have moons. After long periods of searching the Aorgturians found that Earth's chemical and physical make up was very close to their own planet. From the recorded history and modern time observation, the planet is still there. Their planet was three times bigger than Earth with two moons but a warmer climate. It had vast landmasses and oceans, and extensive forest areas to purify their environment.

The Aorgturians were a water loving species requiring warm, moist climates for their survival. They had evolved from a water reptilian species to walk on their lands. Over a few million years they evolved into a highly intelligent, forward-thinking ascended species. They were a tall race with webbed hands and feet with three fingers and toes, and a self-adapting breathing system for water and air. Unlike many species, they did not wear garments, as their bodies could self-regulate temperature within the planet's atmosphere from cold to hot. But they did prefer the heat.

Their science progressed, allowing them to develop multidimensional travel with their physical being and spaceships through the continuum balance of space. Once, they had been a warring species that developed into a peaceful oneness to survive. But because of their recognition that their own planet might not sustain them forever, they sought other planets for future survival. They built a beautiful, vast underwater city on Earth which spread onto the lower lands. It was made up of beautiful structures; their building materials were strong with the appearance of crystal and glass. They could manifest their buildings from their own source of minerals and with help from the Earth's mineral elements.

They occupied Earth in their large city for just under 50,000 Earth years, staying separate from the Earth's creatures and the developing primitive humanoid population as they did not want to influence the planet's natural course of evolution. But I see in the science files held by the Intergalactic Council from this time that they took living samples of many of the creatures to observe.

The knowledge libraries show the Aorgturians eventually found a new home planet, which was not Earth. They too have now perished, never reaching that full state of fifth dimensional ethereal ascension that prolongs life for a near eternal existence. It is funny to think that a lot of the species we will mention no longer exist, but they are not lost forever; thankfully, the universal knowledge library was created by the overseers to store records of their existence and all extinct civilisations and creatures.

Life Journal – transmission 8
New Earth - The light beyond the horizon

Freylen and myself are very excited this light day as I am going to show her one of the magical parts of our planet. We feel it's good to take a break from study to recharge our senses.

I am going to take her to the Mountains Alcerian Touliza, which means crystal light and lakes, which will be a much appreciated delight for our senses. There were times when we lived mainly under the surface of our planet, a circumstance caused by a phenomenon called the Zelicann. It was triggered by a shift in one of our moons after an small asteroid hit it. The moons affect the weather patterns on our planet, so when this one was disrupted it caused this new weather phenomenon to occur. It happened every hundred light days or so, and usually lasted anything from five to ten light days. The light shows and swirling colours of the cloud's storms were hypnotic but would send unpredictable heavy bursts of energy and moisture to the planet's surface, making it hard to live on. As well as affecting the weather pattern it also it affected the energies of the planet, plant life, creatures and the Diacuratians themselves.

This was over eleven thousand hyons ago and as we have ascended in mind and technology, we built beautiful cities, half underground, with large biosphere dome covers for protection. They are scattered around the planet and the domes create the biosphere for existence of balanced pure energy for us to live in. We have also received help from the other civilisations that are part of the Intergalactic Council, and they have helped develop our technology to where we are now, aiding our development and survival. Technology has been given to us that has stabilised our planetary weather system, and the weather pattern is safe once again. Yes, we still have storms, but normal moisture content has returned, and our waterways have returned to normal levels. This has enabled us to slowly move to the surface for living space and agriculture with confidence that no harm will come to our planet's animals or us.

We were very excited as we set off in our travel craft; we had chosen to leave early and get there before the light star was rising. This was because I wanted Freylen to experience the light show from the mountain's crystal formation, which is triggered by the light and warmth of the light star.

We chose a landing site by the largest lake with the mountains as the backdrop. We did not have to wait long to see the star light rays climb up the mountainside; as this happened the rock crystals changed colours and sparkled with colours of purple, lilac and blue mixed with silvers and the white of the mountain. As the light star rays hit the crystals, they absorb the light and reflect their colours back into our world as light beams – it is a spectacular sight to behold; its beauty mesmerised Freylen and it's at moments like this that I realise what a beautiful planet we have.

It was a perfect day weather wise, which allowed swimming in the lake and relaxing on the land. This gave us a chance to get to know each other better and Freylen told me about her family and something of their culture.

She explained there are seven light stars in her home star systems and her people inhabit six planets spread throughout them. Their race has various ascension levels from the physical form to ethereal light beings and there is variation in gene type and consciousness levels as well. As I look at Freylen I see a beautiful, fine-featured slim creature with long, straight, silver blond hair over an elongated head with a pale white skin. She is a highly intelligent, compassionate being with a great sense of humour. She explained their looks can vary, just as the modern Earth populations do with variation in skin colour, height and shape. As to language, it used to vary but now with telepathic connections, they have learnt a light universal language all can understand for their ascension.

Three of the planets are lived on by the ascended physical humanoid beings in the fifth dimension, while three are the base for the ethereal and multidimensional beings of their race. They have a supreme light council made up of twelve light beings that oversee the Pleiadian culture and laws.

Her planet is called Argrian, which means green jewel. She explained it as a water and plant based planet, with a physical humanoid population. She described the beautiful, majestic cities with vast green recreational areas. Her eyes expressed such happiness as she described this idyllic utopia among the stars. Another planet she visits frequently in her system is a healing planet. It is barren, but has amazing lay line energy fields, where they have built pyramids. The pyramids are used for healing and communication with other Pleiadians. On the healing planet, they also work with a race of beings called Hikiconyti. This race is peace-loving, travelling the universe and seeking asylum from their war-torn galaxy. The Pleiadians gave them shelter on the healing planet as the atmosphere suited their physical makeup. They became the overseers of this amazing network of pyramids and buildings, aiding with all healing. Their appearance is quite different to the Pleiadians; the Hikiconyti are very tall, thin beings, grey in colour, their movement being very graceful, and their faces show nothing but kindness to all they meet. Freylen tells me this planet is a Mecca throughout the universe now for healing and learning about these energies.

I understood that all the Pleiadian planets varied slightly, which creates a variant in the Pleiadian race in physical and mind form. Freylen described to me a time of unrest in her peoples; some of them strayed from the light and did not agree with decisions made by the majority and the twelve Pleiadian overseers.

One example she gave was Earth; they have observed the planet from her beginning, estimated 626 billion years ago on Earth's timeline. They have brought their people to Earth to live among them to bring change, especially to the tribes of Native Indians around the Earth. This was so they could be taught the spiritual way to connect with the Mother Earth. But some Pleiadians did not agree with helping other planets and interbreeding, including Earth, and there was interstellar fighting for a long time. But eventually the light won over the darkness and their people learnt from this dark period in their history to live in peace with each other.

In the most recent period of Earth's history I see they still walk among the Earth humans, in physical beings as incarnated souls. Their mission is to help Earth ascend to a state of consciousness where there is no harm to others and their planet Mother Earth.

After a wonderful day, my pleasure was enhanced when I arrived back at my dwelling to find a message from Baltrexn. He was heading back to the Diacurat space station estimating ten light days to his arrival. He had been out of mind-to-mind connection for a few light days due to the galaxy they were visiting. It was most likely I would have to go to the space station to see him, but I would find out more on his return.

Life Journal – transmission 9
New Earth - The light beyond the horizon

Earth had been left alone for two million years after the Aorgturians. As we both studied the next phase of Earth's history, we went forward to the time when an Earth subspecies developed into the primitive upright form of early humanoid beings. The species now had primitive intelligence and was physically well adapted to Earth's atmosphere. This new species drew the attention of the overseers back to Earth and the possibility of it being used as an experimental base. Their thoughts were to mix DNA from star beings with the subspecies to create a more intelligent humanoid form. This would lead to study and a possible base of the incarnation program working on Earth in the future.

The planet had suffered yet another ice age in this time period. An ice age is caused by collective effects of changes in the Earth's movements on its climate over thousands of years, where regular changes in the Earth's tilt and orbit combine to affect the areas on Earth which get more or less light star solar radiation. When all these factors align and the northern hemisphere gets less solar radiation in summer, an ice age can be started. It can also be triggered by an asteroid strike or human technology and weapons knocking Mother Earth out of alignment. By the time the primitive human species was developing, the Earth was recovering from the ice age and the planet's energies were more settled.

With the overseers leading the program, the Intergalactic Council selected Earth as an experimental platform for what was called humanoid life. From a small group of primate forms they wanted to create a new humanoid form that had spontaneous association of ideas, and would encourage cooperation in group living with a protective consciousness of ego. The free will ego would allow for control and self-preservation, leading to leadership for survival of their kind. This led them to experiment with DNA from a couple of star species to start this chain of events. The star species were Lemurians and Anunnkai, humanoid forms similar in makeup to the DNA of Earth's primates, but more highly formed, intelligent and ascended beings.

They were both chosen for different reasons. The Lemurians come from the Earth's galaxy on a planet of similar structure and type. This peaceful, beautiful race of highly intelligent humanoids had observed Earth for a long time and felt influencing the new humanoid species might lead them to eventually colonise Earth themselves. The Anunnkai were a different energy race, more aggressive in nature with a large, strong physical form that had a passion for power and riches. But saying that their intelligence allowed them not to want to harm another species or planet. They were invited to the Intergalactic Council due to this ethos of thinking. They travelled from their home system on a rogue planet where they had built a base. They controlled the planet with advanced technology; I discovered in the universe's knowledge library that it is very unusual to use a rogue planet in this way. The Anunnkai also had an interest in Earth for future inhabitation, which explains why they were keen to be involved. So, the two contrasting DNAs were used for the first humanoid experiment on Earth, and were observed from afar.

No humanoid form at this stage on Earth had an incarnated soul, but every human has what we all call the human essence energy of who they are. On death in this ancient time period, this energy returned to their planet and the universal energy source.

The experiment was created so new younglings were born with the enhanced DNA sequence and then they were left alone while their development was studied. The outcome at this early stage was that two groups of humanoids formed – one that stayed untouched by the experiment, allowing the Earth primate to evolve naturally, and the new enhanced species, which was noticeably the more advanced in intelligence and had different features.

Over thousands of years the new humanoid species was left to develop, during which time it migrated over the developing continents. Some did breed with the lesser species, adding a third element to the mix and complicating the results. The experiment also had to cope with Earth's forever changing climate and glacial disruptions. During this experimental time, there were also further outside influences from other star species.

Now some of you might think, as I did at first, that interfering with the natural evolution of a planet is not a very loving way to behave. Freylen also said her people had been involved in many of Earth's experiments along her timeline, always with the intention of enhancing the societies on Earth for ascension. The overseers always looked for ways to enhance planets and species, and as in all branches of science, you need test subjects to learn from. All the Earth experiments I reveal are for the intended advancement of its humanoids, and were created for the good of the planet.

I also realised that Diacurat was an early experiment for the overseers when they gave us the knowledge crystal. We were left to ascend on our own with this knowledge, with our free will and ego learning to come into balance. I know they only choose planets they feel have the early signs of the right frequency spiritual energy, and Earth was evolving in this way. I knew I had to respect the millions of hyons of the overseers' high knowledge, always seeking the noblest and best outcome for all. I also realised that there are darker forces at work too, that tried to hinder their influences on the universe.

At the end of another long light day I am pleased to say I am off tomorrow's light day to see my bonded partner Baltrexn on the planet's space station. We have already had very personal mind contact now he's back in our galaxy. But there is nothing like the physical contact of flesh to flesh to seal the bond of love as life partners.

Life Journal – transmission 10
New Earth - The light beyond the horizon

This light day started off with more excitement than usual, as I readied myself to travel by portal to the space station to see Baltrexn. The station is called Calparieon, meaning high night star. It is a rotating circular structure, with a hole in the centre and six tower spikes above and below the main structure. There are various sections such as living quarters for crew and visitors, docking and portal stations, science, engineering and observation sections. I often see it in our night dark sky as it passes over the planet. I often wonder about all the species that visit and what is happening on this hub of life above us.

I arrived at the station and saw Baltrexn waiting for me; we embraced each other, not worrying about what others might see or feel. We had been apart for too long and longed just to be with each other in the peace of our energy. As we walked to his quarters, I saw lots of different species, some not familiar to me, and resolved that I would ask more about them later. Firstly, we needed to catch up and bond our energy again to feel as one.

Baltrexn was too busy to come down to Diacurat this time as they were heading out again in a couple of light days. We knew when we life bonded there would be long periods apart, although I only find it hard when we cannot communicate via mind or communication frequencies through space. Some of his missions take him off to far reaches of the universe; when this happens, communication has a delay in space-time, as time of movement varies throughout the universe.

As well as treating any crew members, he has to learn about the anatomy of any new species that they connect with through the Intergalactic Council.

A lot of these species will not come down to the surface of Diacurat as they often use the station as a stopover on the way to other places, or a study point.

We spent a lovely evening with some of Baltrexn's friends, where I met another Pleiadian call Siroian who knew Freylen, so she joined us. It was a fascinating evening, enjoying being with different cultures from across the planetary systems. I stayed the night in his ship's quarters, enjoying our time together. The next light day Baltrexn had duties to attend to, so we arranged to meet up again in the evening, when his parents were joining us.

Baltrexn's parents were a lovely bonded couple; they were teachers and taught our culture's history to the younglings. They were very proud of what Baltrexn had achieved in his medical career so far and they also missed his energy being around them. I had yet another lovely evening catching up with everyone but felt a pang of sadness that our short time together was soon to end.

Life Journal – transmission 11
New Earth - The light beyond the horizon'

As I sit on my own, staring out at the lake our dwelling looks out on to, I am reflecting on my goodbyes to Baltrexn. It does not get any easier, but I am grateful for my work and my Earth studies that distract me while he is away. I am just waiting for Freylen to arrive so we can start our light day's work and have our morning meal.

When she arrived, we discussed the night before, and how she knew Siroian. When I mentioned him, to my surprise Freylen looked quite coy and a little flustered, realising she had a strong liking for this handsome Pleiadian. She revealed he knew her older sibling brother and they had been educated together back on her home planet. Siroian was part of the science crew of a star ship delegation from the Pleiadians. They travelled to various planets and space stations visiting their own kind, collecting data and being placed where they were needed for added support. Apparently, they had had an intimate moment last night and he would endeavour to return soon, and they were going to stay mind linked. As Freylen was going to be with me for a while it limited her ability to go and visit him.

I have always believed that meetings are not coincidence and from my seeing Baltrexn, they met up again after all this time. I do love it when two beautiful beings come together and there is that possible spark of love there.

Well after all that excitement we are back on track with our studying. Now I mentioned the Lemurians and Anunnkai earlier, for your information; they both show up in the modern Earth's folklore history in a mythical capacity. Every other species we have mentioned is not recorded by the humans in Earth's known human or modern history. A lot of Earth's history is recorded on old monument walls and is deciphered by modern man creating a legend. This legend then creates a myth and myths create a story told, and many retell them over the centuries and the truth is lost in the retelling of the stories.

But before I reveal their timelines on Earth, I want to enlighten you about when the incarnation program started on Earth. A few thousand years after the DNA upgrade for the new humanoid form, it was considered a success and the new species were showing the desired collectiveness in groups for survival. The overseers decided this would be a good planet on which to extend the incarnation program to, so many of the universe's species could experience this new creation and how it unfolds. It was also felt that over time it was an ideal planet to hold further experiments with the human form due to its energy and position in the galaxy, which was easily accessible. So, the go-ahead was given for Earth to join the incarnation program. The Intergalactic Council selected the Lemurians as the first candidates for this. They were the most experienced at this process, and when they were successful on Earth, others would be allowed to be part of this experiment over time. At this early stage there was no thought of helping these humanoids see the light and ascend, they just wanted to keep it simple until it was established. So the purpose was simply for incarnated beings to experience this Earth experiment from a different perspective. The data from the incarnation experiences would be collated together for assessment to help future decisions on the Earth planet.

The Anunnkai, as called by modern Earth humanoids, came to the planet in their full physical form in the Earth time period of around 450,000 BC. We know them as the Tyrangions but will use Anunnkai for Earth's decoding language. The Lemurians in the period of 250,000 BC were again being selected for their DNA for the first Atlantis experiment humanoids. They would also continue in the incarnation program on Earth and into the future.

First of all, I will cover the Anunnkai (Tyrangion) period of Earth history for your interest. After observing the planet for 200,000 years they decided to come and live among the humans that had had their DNA altered. They chose an area of land inhabited by these humanoids in the warm regions of Earth. They had an ulterior motive, which was to mine gold and the rich minerals they needed for their own manifestation of objects as they travelled the universe. Compared to the Earth humans they were a good three feet taller and very heavyset, strong beings. The male of the species was dominant, and the females were subservient to them. They came from the far reaches of space from a system known to us as Tyrangion. This was linked with an unusual format of three small light stars and their home world was part of this system. They had mastered their technology for space travel a long time ago with great understanding of the power of light, colour and harmonic sound frequencies. They had a small rogue planet come through their system that got caught up in their light stars' orbits, not causing any real harm. They decided to build an off-world space station on this planet and create through advanced technology a way of controlling the frequencies of the rogue planet for space travel.

This is the first time I have known about this type of space travel as I study this subject, but Freylen already knew of other species doing this too. I see they could use portals of space matter to jump to various galaxies throughout the universe. They used their technology to balance each solar system as they passed through or stopped, so the rogue planet did not affect the existing gravitational energy's pull of light stars or planets. I love it when I discover something new; we never limit ourselves by restricting our thoughts, as there are so many possibilities in our universe.

When looking at Earth's history, it records the Anunnaki as deities who appear in the mythological traditions of the ancient Sumerians. As history unfolded the Sumerians were considered the creators of civilisation, as modern humans tried to understand them and the evidence left behind. They were one of the first advanced civilisations to appear on Earth in this experimental phase created by the Anunnaki. They built an empire of twelve cities that were walled metropolises. These cities were dominated by tiered pyramid temples, which were used for healing and worship. A complex astronomical and astrological system was created that incorporated the movements and qualities of numerous celestial bodies. They used the pyramids to teach and align to the stars for knowledge. This created the celestial method of knowledge for sea travel and crop harvesting linking to the sun, moon and the seasons. This shows up around the Earth in many future civilisations. In fact, it served as the marker by which life on the planet became ordered, as it contained information crucial to life, such as the movements and interrelationship of the sun and moon.

The Anunnaki showed the humanoids how to farm and build homes to create a more advanced civilisation. They taught the humans about mining so they could gather the precious ores and minerals they needed for their own objective – aiding their materialisation processes. They were a strong force to deal with and the humanoid beings were very subservient and fearful at first. But as the years progressed and the humanoid intelligence grew with these gods from the sky, a better understanding and mutual respect grew between them.

During this time period of growth as relationships between the humans and Anunnaki became stronger, some the Anunnaki took human women to mate with, creating a new hybrid species among the humans. The Anunnaki stayed on Earth for just under four thousand years, finally wishing to return to their home world with the knowledge gleaned from their travels. Some of the humans they had mated with along with their offspring went with them, as they were now considered family. They also left behind hybrids who mated with other humans after their occupation of Earth. When the Anunnaki left, the humans floundered for a while, many not coping without the hierarchy and intelligence of the Anunnaki. This led them to deserting the cities and regressing to more nomadic behaviour. But many managed to retain some of the basic farming knowledge they had been given, which was passed to future generations. They also had a greater understanding of the sky and celestial bodies. As the mythical history shows on Earth, the Anunnaki said they would return one day; at the moment they will not be allowed to make a physical presence again, but may continue to observe Earth from afar.

As we move towards the next big event on Earth, the Atlantis period, I am very excited, as this was the era Touliza our incarnation program founder entered as an incarnated soul.

Life Journal – transmission 12
New Earth - The light beyond the horizon

This light day I met again with Havrium from my incarnation team at the mind and body travel institute and Freylen was also invited. Havrium wanted to see how we were progressing with our Earth studies and if we had any questions. I had one so far: I was curious about who my network of support would be when I incarnate. These are fellow beings who will guide my incarnated life on Earth. As it turned out some thought had been given to this, but was not yet finally decided. The general feeling was they wanted some guides with previous Earth incarnation experience. Freylen put herself forward for a guide role and Havrium graciously said he would consider her.

After our meeting we took advantage of the light day and went to the Alcerian Touliza Creatorion to see a new art exhibition. The Creatorion was built by Zogica, the famous Touliza's bond partner. This amazing structure is a timeless piece of art itself and stands proudly among many of our finest structures on Diacurat. The art show we wanted to see was by a Diacurat artist called Flizya, an artist who used the light and sound frequencies to create art images that float and move around the space in the room. You can interact with these images and they react to your own energy signatures. It was fascinating to see as a lot of the images reflected off-world creatures we had never seen before.

We then took time to wander around the beautiful grounds and gardens, settling by a water fountain to enjoy lunch and the space around us. Our conversation soon came around to our Earth studies as we are both enjoying this experience so much.

We cheerfully headed back to my dwelling to start our next study session.

After the Anunnaki left Earth it was agreed to leave all the humanoids to exist without interference from a supreme race, leaving them to naturally evolve until the Intergalactic Council intervened again. They would have incarnated souls as we mentioned earlier, so other species could observe and experience the more primitive, heavier existence of the 3D matrix.

It was not until around 250,000 BC that the Earth took on a new dimensional existence which involved the first of the Atlantis experiments – there were five in total. Now the Earth word 'experiment' does not fully describe the reasoning behind the events on Earth as we go forward. The Earth word 'experiment' is defined as a procedure carried out to support, refute, or validate a hypothesis from the mind. Experiments provide insight into cause and effect by demonstrating what outcome occurs when a particular factor or factors are manipulated. Experiments vary greatly in goal and scale, but always rely on repeatable procedure and logical analysis of the results.

To the ascension being behind Earth's history as we go forward, the experiment was to try different options of existence to learn from, so the overseers improved upon their knowledge for future generations of all beings in the universe. The free choice for the physical humanoid was not always there. The higher self of the incarnated soul chooses their life path for the incarnated experience, learning to deal with the human's developing ego and essence of free will.

The divine creators, the overseers and the Intergalactic Council, with its mission to bring a spiritual existence with love and kindness to all in the universe, triggered these experiment ideas. They wanted a centre point for the experiment, which would be an exchange centre for information, a light centre of this living cosmic library of knowledge. I use the word cosmic, as beings from far and wide were at intervals invited to view these experiments and gather their own observations. They would bring their knowledge back to the Intergalactic Council, the overseers and their own civilisations. Earth was used to see if various high-ascended energy beings could incarnate within the physical humanoid body and maintain the high source link of the divine creative energy. The core of this was to see how information could be stored through frequencies and the genetic process. If successful, the experiment would pave the way to helping other lower energy planets and civilisations survive, ascend and thrive. They would incarnate into these beings, bringing the unconditional love energy, and wait for the spark of the high spiritual pure love to be recognised, which would lead to starting the ascension process. So, from what we could see, there was a lot riding on the success of these Atlantis experiments.

The first three Atlantis experiments were between the Earth dates 250,000 BC to 52,000 BC. For the first experiment the master scientists of the Intergalactic Council created a new, highly intelligent physical humanoid species. This new physical human species could survive in the lower energy allowing the higher ascended spirit energy to incarnate into them. The new humanoids were tall with very pale blue grey skin, high foreheads, blue eyes and blond hair. The new DNA came from four high-ascended species in the universe compatible with the Earth humanoid DNA. It had to be from species that still took physical form, so the Lemarutarian, Pleiadian, Arcturian and Andromedan peoples were chosen. The DNA was already charged with high consciousness, as the aim of the experiment was to create a physical form suitable for incarnation by a highly ascended ethereal form. The ones chosen to incarnate were aware, while in their physical form of their mission on Earth to create and sustain a highly ascended utopian culture, which other ethereal beings could incarnate into. These physical human beings could live for around 150 or more Earth years and radiated out their pure energy. This was because of the healing light energy that sustains the incarnated being (known as soul or inner spirit on Earth).

In the first Atlantis experiment, there was no sex gender in the new Earth species; they reproduced by the conscious mind. To keep the populations going, the Intergalactic Council provided humans on Earth when required. The Council wanted to keep it simple at the start, monitoring the physical body reaction to an incarnated soul. So, these human beings did not know physical love as those in future experiments did. The Council also chose to create the cities and living areas on a warm southern landmass. There was a well-balanced ecosystem for survival among the Earth species at the time. The Council also introduced animals from some of the incarnated home worlds – such as winged horses and exotic flying creatures, which, as spiritual beings in their own right, were treated as equals. The Council was very keen to create a spiritual environment on Earth where they would be controlled so no other outside influence could interfere. They created a life of utopia with no materialistic values, and all actions taken were for the whole.

This new Earth human species for the first Atlantis experiment was called Lemurian, after the Lemurians who incarnated into the new Earth beings. They were selected for this first experiment due to their study involvement on the subject. As time progressed and the first experiment proved to be a success, they also eventually selected other ethereal beings to join them and contribute. Other highly evolved human form beings connected with the Intergalactic Council came to visit the Earth beings. Word soon got out into the universe of these experiments and caused a lot of interest, which led to curious spectators, some of these arriving in star ships, others by teleportation through the dimension's light way portals. The experiment was a huge success, but these new visitors influenced them over time as their thoughts and behaviour brought a different way of thinking, leaving their mark on the once pure thinking Atlantean society.

For the second experiment they introduced mixed gender, creating a beautiful race of beings living in beautiful cities within a utopian lifestyle. Earth did not pose many threats, as they fortified their boundaries to keep the outside world at bay. They had flying machines and sea boats to explore the world, not really showing any thought of how they might affect the lower energy populations if they were seen. As far as I can see from the knowledge preserved, change came when they allowed visits to Atlantis by other off-world beings again. This brought new influences on the physical beings and changed their outlook on life. Over thousands of years the Atlantean humans developed their own self-essence, developing ego and self-preservation, which led to a breakdown in this utopian society.

On the third experiment they had mixed genders again, the master scientists this time choosing to guide the third experiment humans, connecting the volunteer prior to being incarnated. Previously this had not been the case, and they now wanted to change the spiritual base to the experiment. They decided some should stay single for the roles of priest and priestess in the light temples, and that these humans would be more highly evolved with greater consciousness. The physical bonding love was seen as an act of pure connection, with the result of new life to be highly valued. Again, this was all overseen by the Intergalactic Council, which influenced the DNA of these people born to Earth. The humans this time round were also highly intelligent, but the DNA was diversified again, as in the second experiment, to produce individual beings as opposed to the identical beings of the first experiment. The plan was that human appearance would become more varied than the second experiment through the new generations.

In each of the three experiments, some of the human forms developed strong egos, and this energy affected the incarnated souls as time passed. The soul was still connected to the higher self, but the human ego caused them to lose sight of the mission, and their energies became heavier. Over time, humans realised their own powers could influence others of their race, and an avaricious way of being came about, resulting in a materialistic and greedy reality. With each new generation, the humans distanced themselves from the high-energy pure unconditional love source and their powers weakened.

It came to the point where many of the incarnated beings in humans, who were still in the high energy, did not wish to stay on Earth, because they knew it would end in a breakdown in society and self-destruction. So they were given the choice to finish their experience in the human form on Earth or vacate the physical body and return to their home existence. Many did choose to leave the experiment. This, combined with the breakdown of the rest of the Atlantean society, contributed to the failure of the first three Atlantis experiments, with all ending in similar fates.

The archive shows each time that an experiment self-destructed; the Council left a time period of settlement before trying again. Two failed attempts followed by a third caused the overseers to put a stop to these experiments for a while and ask the Intergalactic Council to revaluate what it was trying to achieve. After the destruction of the cities, the third experiment ended with allowing an asteroid to hit the Earth, triggering an extinction event eliminating all traces of the Atlantean technology. They felt it was time to re-cleanse the planet and let her be for a few thousand years to find her pure frequency again. Some Atlantean humanoids chose to survive, mingling with the other Earth humans who were not part of the Atlantean experiments and who survived the extinction event, and were left to naturally evolve again.

When the overseers felt Earth was balanced again it was decided to start a fourth Atlantis experiment in 28,000 BC, which lasted 10,000 years. The new Atlantean society was spread across a large landmass by the warm seas in the southern hemisphere – a green, lush, fertile environment connecting with the sea, with golden sands and fresh land waters. The Intergalactic Council ensured there were the resources to build cities and thrive. The new early Atlanteans in the fourth experiment built their own cities, travel routes and a temple for their high light council. This new Atlantis society had a high council made up of priests and priestesses with the knowledge needed to support their society. They also had a direct link to the divine source and the Intergalactic Council;

with this, they taught the new Earth human volunteers who came forward for this role about the 'Law of One'. There were also smaller temples, where the new priests and priestesses who volunteered were known as 'The Ones of the Light'. From these beautiful temples they brought physical and mental healing to the Atlantean people, maintaining the high energy needed for the success of the experiment.

The Intergalactic Council decided again that the physical human would be created in male and female form, reproducing through physical contact. They also decided that life would not be as comfortable as in previous experiments, which made the fourth Atlantis experiment more of a challenge. The humans were downloaded with the practical skills of survival, but also with the psychic energy needed that would give them a chance to achieve oneness with each other and the Earth. Their DNA was similar to that of the third experiment, but this time they added some new energy strands from the light beings of Salcariton. The DNA can alter in regenerations of the physical forms to higher or lower frequencies, depending on the species' development. The ascended masters could switch off the frequencies if they wanted a lower energy being, and turn them up if they required a being with a higher energy frequency. So they conducted trials to try and find a suitable balance in each experiment. They hoped they had it right this time. The new Earth humanoid also had the twelve chakras energy points to help maintain the physical and mind connection to the divine source and the planet.

The Salcaritons were from the ninth dimension, raised above the Sirius region of the universe – another high-ascended ethereal race that the overseers invited to the fourth experiment. When not in physical form their DNA is what we call star DNA, an injection of their ethereal energy. These spiritual beings existed in a blissful heavenly utopia plane of oneness in unconditional love. The Salcaritons had mastered incarnation in lower level energy species from the second-dimension levels to the fifth. They stopped here, as when a being has reached the fifth level it no longer needs the light soul within, as it had itself become the light creating multidimensional form. They were and still are a wonderful asset to the Intergalactic Council and the continuing Earth experiments.

The Lemurians also decided to continue to incarnate, as by now they had the building blocks within to improve on the learning some of them had failed previously to attain. Towards the end of the first 5,000 years the fourth experiment began to wobble. The same pattern emerged as before, and the Intergalactic Council tried hard to inject love and light into the experiment. They introduced high-energy loving animals from other planets, such as cats, elephants, giraffes and dolphins, and invited further ascended energy beings to reincarnate. This helped for a while but slowly the heavier lower energy again took hold.

At the end of the fourth experiment there was mass destruction as the low energy factions turned against each other in the fight for supremacy. They had developed technology that involved high-energy weapons penetrating deep into the Earth's core. These weapons caused the planet great harm in her core and atmosphere, and this time she reacted by flipping her axis, trying to cleanse herself of the pollution and negative energy. This caused landmasses to move, a mini ice age was created on earth, and the temperature dropped across sixty percent of its surface, killing plant life and many mammals and humans. Most of the evidence of the fourth Atlantis experiment and previous experiments was destroyed.

Surviving humans, mainly in the southern hemispheres, carried on in small pockets of communities. They were now a mixture of original humans, what was left from the four Atlantis experiments. As the planet healed, these humans spread to other areas over time to create small civilisations. The Salcaritons chose to keep incarnating in these Earth humans as a support system, helping to raise the planet's energies in the event of another Atlantis experiment. They tried to guide the people to a simple spiritual existence, respecting animals and Mother Earth as they now called her.

The knowledge archives show there was confusion among the Intergalactic Council members as to why these experiments kept failing, and what was triggering the humans to sink into lower energies. The master scientists were busy trying to find out what went wrong – was it DNA deterioration, or humans' minds somehow changing frequency, being influenced from some unseen source? The Salcaritons were confused too, as they thought they had mastered this, but some of their incarnated human physical forms also strayed into the lower Earth energies.

We are both finding this Atlantis history on Earth so interesting! I reveal here the basic outline of events, and the testimonials from the knowledge Touzlia left us in 'The light within Atlantis' section will reveal more to you.

Life Journal – transmission 13
New Earth - The light beyond the horizon

As we reach the final stage of the Atlantis experiments, we can reveal knowledge of experiment number five in Earth year 11,500 BC, documenting some very interesting events over its 1550 Earth years. After the four failed Atlantis experiments, the overseers and Intergalactic Council chose to have one final attempt. They decided to create a new Atlantis and populate it with new humanoid forms of gender, male and female, but chose to change their DNA sequence again.

They asked the Salcaritons to review the DNA, and their findings showed that when linked with the chakras, it was too weak in frequency to maintain the fifth dimensional link against the dark energies. The DNA needed to be structured to support a strong link with a self-adjusting frequency to maintain balance. With their knowledge of studying many species in the universe, they adjusted the new human DNA to a twelve helix DNA that had previously worked well in other situations. This was a high frequency system that would stay activated while the physical human was connected to the divine light source. With the twelve chakras and this high frequency DNA, the Atlanteans were able to live in a five-dimensional status within the Earth's three dimensional energy field. With this unified combination of DNA and chakras they were psychic, with clairsentience, clairaudience and clairvoyance abilities. This enabled telekinesis, which powered them to use their minds to manifest material substance and manipulate it by drawing on the high consciousness cosmic matrix. They were the most physically and mentally powerful of all the humanoids yet developed.

Up to this point they had been recreating the human species, but now they decided that if the fifth experiment failed, they would let the Atlantean humans that chose to stay, spread around Earth and live their lives, watching how new societies developed. In other words, they were already planning a sixth experiment as a fallback. The Salcaritons would oversee this sixth experiment and be the main incarnated souls among the humans. They would also carefully select other high-status beings to incarnate. This would depend on how the Earth progressed, and whether it would need redirection towards the unconditional love energy source again.

They also built into their high frequency DNA the knowledge and instincts for survival, how to build their own homes and temples through mind materialisation, and how to live on Earth's land. They made Earth part of their energy connection as well as staying connected to the higher energy light source of the divine overseers. They created a beautiful race of people, tall with blond hair, blue eyes, olive skin, and great clear-seeing intelligence. Built into the DNA were variants such as hair and eye colour that would show in future generations, creating a race of individuals. The humanoid form would also maintain the telepathic abilities and telekinesis, and some would also have teleporting skills.

There were more primitive humans on the planet who survived the mini ice age, some of these were descendants of survivors from the previous experiments who were living in small communities. Because of their isolation, they had learned to live peacefully, helped by the influence of the Salcaritons' incarnations, which had continued throughout this interesting phase of Earth's climate adjustment as she renewed and cleansed herself.

The decision regarding where to base the new Atlantis was influenced by how the Earth was healing after the mini ice age, since the landmasses in some northern areas were still settling and regenerating. Because of this, they decided that the main Atlantis city would be sited on a large, separate landmass, which was again in the warm southern hemisphere. This was now a stable environment, and only future positive energy growth was foreseen. The master scientists made sure the chosen lands had what was needed to build temples and homes, with a sustainable supply of food and fresh water. They built twelve cities in total around the Earth in habitable areas and all had temples. Following advice from the Salcaritons, they decided that the temples should be built over the energy lines that run through and round the planet, so they could tap into its power. This would connect the physical beings to Earth's pure energy and help keep her balanced. It would also help the Earth chakra energy to give grounding strength, helping to balance the multidimensional energies.

The temples were pyramids of sacred geometry and stunning architecture, many of them covered in a dome of projected crystalline amplified energy light that looked like a glowing force field. The energy fields projected above the temples were of various colours, according to the purpose of them, and glowed day and night like the Aurora seen on Earth. The main city of Atlantis had an approximate Earth measurement of fourteen miles before its demise. The city was designed with the temple of light in the centre, set on high ground to overlook the land.

The methodology of the fifth experiment had been altered, so in the first phase, the Intergalactic Council did not supply the materials for the building of the cities. The humans learned to pull together to build their structures, using Earth's natural resources and the materialisation gift to create whatever else was needed to aid the process. The master scientists made sure the landmasses they inhabited provided all they needed. Their water came from freshwater wells in each city, and there were central lakes and bathing areas for communities to enjoy. They also loved gardens, waterfalls and fountains as this energy provided a peaceful spiritual area for recharging the human form.

The evidence shows this was successful, as they helped build each other's homes and worked for the whole not for the one, which kept them in the high frequency energy. In the beginning, it was an existence of simplicity, maintaining the divine connection and making sure all needs were met in the love and light energy. As time went on the inhabitants built more refined homes, using gold, bronze, copper and gems for internal and exterior decoration. The social structure became more civilised and they managed to retain their elevated energy connection needed for the experiment not to fail. The arts like painting and music prevailed, with buildings and institutions dedicated to these pursuits. The children were nurtured so they could reach their best potential and find their true-life path amongst their people.

An interesting piece of information is that in the other four experiments, the humans' incarnated souls all knew each other before they incarnated. The Intergalactic Council had set up a college of experiment called 'The School of Light', where all chosen beings could gather to learn about the new human form and what they could expect when they incarnated. Each time a new generation was needed, the selected beings would familiarise themselves with each other at 'The School of Light' before incarnating into the Atlanteans. In the fourth experiment, they even chose their bonding mates before they came to Earth.

For the fifth experiment, they chose to close the school and the participants did not meet any other beings before incarnating except their guiding mission team. This practice, which has stayed the same and is still the benchmark throughout the universe, was adopted on the recommendation of the Salcaritons. They felt the Intergalactic Council should properly challenge this experiment to get the fullest information from the results, hopefully giving answers to why some parts were successful and past experiments eventually failed. Individually, the beings to incarnate were familiarised with the human form on their home planet or realm, with members of the Intergalactic Council assisting, the process I am going through at the moment. I see they really wanted to test the waters this time and felt confident that with the Salcaritons' newfound science on incarnation, they could afford to introduce more change to the boundaries of the experiment.

When the fifth Atlantis experiment was created, the Intergalactic Council decided to house twelve cosmic beings from the tenth dimension, in a star ship held above the centre of the main Atlantis city in Earth's atmosphere. These were highly evolved light beings all connected with the various home planets and realms of those who were incarnating. The star ship was designed to be a temple of light of unconditional love for teaching and knowledge for the Atlantean people. These twelve cosmic beings are called the Celestial Guardians and their role is to oversee the experiment then report back to the Intergalactic Council and the overseers. The star ship also has another vital role; it has a Calentian Crystal that powers the Earth's biosphere domes. The biosphere dome was placed around the cities and lands to protect them from predators and unwanted primitive human contact. The crystal is also a computer that records everything that has happened, like a library of knowledge on Atlantis and its history. The temple of light in central Atlantis had a smaller Calentian Crystal that connected with the higher star ship crystal. The other eleven temples in the other cities also had crystals that interlinked with the main Atlantean light temple crystal and the star ship.

The human population chose priests and priestesses to lead the people in the Twelve Laws and carry out healing among them. The twelve Celestial Guardians only connected to these chosen humans and had no contact with others on Earth. Their purpose was to help the experiment keep its energies on the high frequency required for success.

As time progressed with the fifth experiment, it started to break down, society broke off into fractions, with humans letting ego overrule the soul connection, leading them to seek power over others.

The overseers and Intergalactic Council were confused at the failure of yet another experiment. It was our founder Touliza's incarnated life as the Earth human Aigle, that revealed the reason. A race of dark energy beings, the Derepliticon, had mastered the art of disguising their darker incarnated soul energies, which allowed them to infiltrate the Atlantean beings and cause chaos among the humanoids. This scenario had not even crossed anyone's mind in all the years of the Atlantis experiments, but now it was all starting to make sense.

The Derepliticon race involvement caused all the cities' utopia societies to decline without not much hope of recovery – the balance of lower, heavy energies now outweighed the lighter love energies. The star races involved in the incarnation programme had all agreed that it should end. They had been given the choice of triggering the death of the physical host and collect their incarnated reflective selves, or carry on in the physical form until a natural death occurred on Earth. They had also decided not to do another Atlantis experiment on Earth; the result of this decision would mean that all their powers, crystals, technology and the Celestial Guardians would leave the planet. They also wanted to destroy any buildings using Atlantis technology so it was not handed to any future Earth occupation by dark energies, or a new experiment that might be influenced by it. They asked the humans that chose to stay to vacate the cities to high ground, and then created earthquakes that triggered tsunamis, taking the land and the evidence of Atlantis back to the depths of the seas. But this was not entirely successful, as remains of buildings exist in modern Earth in an area known as Tiwanaku, an archaeological site in western Bolivia, South America. It was part of the Atlantean cities built with technology the primitive humans of that era did not have. Even now, I can see that after thousands of years of erosion, the perfectly shaped stones, intricately routed patterns and perfectly drilled round holes of the ascension Atlantean technology origins are still visible. They chose to leave these few bits of evidence to see how future humanity would interpret them, and whether or not they would accept the reality of powers and beings beyond their three-dimensional existence.

The humans who chose to remain scattered to higher ground for survival, and when it was safe they found new lands to populate, eventually triggering new civilisations over several thousand years.

Life Journal – transmission 14
New Earth - The light beyond the horizon

I hope you are enjoying the transmissions about the Earth's history; we must not lose sight that this knowledge is vital for your own understanding and mine. The time I will incarnate into is a new, cleansed Earth - all the planet's history leads to this point in its timeline. So it's vital to have a deep understanding of how humanity developed, declined and was reborn many times. We have put together a timetable of how humanity went on to develop from small groups into further civilisations around the Earth. From this, we can highlight the further involvement of the Intergalactic Council and other celestial beings.

The humanoids left on Earth were a mix of the original subspecies who developed into the primitive upright form of early humanoid beings, and the humanoids left from many years of experiments, and the hybrid programmes of ascension beings. These two started to spread and merge, helping to create further civilisations on Earth. The northern hemispheres such as Nordic Scandinavia and the Prussian lands were mainly populated from the subspecies humanoids made up from the primitive humans that had had no further interference from the experiments. They were allowed to evolve after the last ice age to present day human history, being vehicles for incarnation and learning. As they learnt to travel and invade other lands, their DNA started to mix with some of the higher ascension humanoids.

Around the Earth time period of 4000 BC a group of humans named the Sumerians (who we mentioned earlier) had developed what was considered by modern humans to be one of the first forward thinking civilisations. They are remembered for their innovations in language, governance, architecture and much more. Modern humans see Sumerians as the creators of civilisation as modern humans understand it. With the help of the Anunnkai they provided the building blocks for other civilisations that lasted two thousand years. Within this time frame the Egyptian empire developed and grew; Freylen has a story to tell about her incarnation on Earth later on in these transmissions.

3100BC – 30 BC Egyptian empire - The dynastic period started with the reign of Egypt's first king, Narmer, in approximately 3100 BC, and ended with the death of Cleopatra VII in 30 BC. During this long period there were times of strong centralised rule, and periods of much weaker, divided rule, but basically Egypt remained one independent land. Throughout the Egyptian rule we have further evidence of the influence of ascension beings and hybrid activity. This was recorded on the walls of temples depicting deities and spacecraft. Part of this wall art shows a caped alien being offered some sort of live fowl. The Egyptian people were also well equipped with deep knowledge and understanding about outer space. There are actually spiral images in the Egyptian hieroglyphics, which symbolise galaxies and their energy. Aside from that, there are images of some half-animal, half-human creatures, as well as reptilian creatures. These are images and symbols of extra-terrestrials who influenced this civilisation. I have discovered that on Earth, there are images from a 3,000-year old 'New Kingdom Temple' in Egypt, which show images of the modern-day submarines and helicopters, as well as something that looks like a spaceship on the ceiling. Funnily enough, I see in modern Earth records that humans with power over their societies hide this information from the viewing public. They do not understand the ascension beings that visited Egypt, or the DNA influence from past high ascension humanoids who survived to pass on these memories.

An ascension race we called Heplearians came to Earth in this time period to aid humanity. They were of human form but a tall handsome race with elongated skulls. The Intergalactic Council allowed their presence as an experiment to see how they could create a civilisation of great standing. They built this on the back of the early Egyptian period where there were signs of intelligence to use as a building platform. Their DNA could be used for hybrid children by mating with the finest Earth women specimens. This was just in the houses of the high rulers and kings; they wanted to create a higher-level ascension humanoid. I do see though that it caused some to die at a young age and the compatibility was not as strong as they hoped for. This race brought healing ways, astrologic knowledge and the secret of pyramids from their home world. During this period, they also influenced other civilisations on Earth, giving their knowledge to aid them in manifesting great things from the human mind – the Indus and Maya being the two main races to benefit from this knowledge.

3300 BC - 1900 BC - The Indus Valley Civilisation is in an area called South Asia. They were allowed to thrive, developing intelligence for their urban planning, baked brick houses, elaborate drainage systems, water supply systems, clusters of large non-residential buildings, and new techniques in handicrafts.

2000 BC - 1600 AD - The Maya civilisation developed within a region that spreads from the modern Earth region of northern Mexico, southwards into Central America. They developed a sophisticated and highly developed writing system as well as art, architecture, mathematics, a calendar, and an astronomical theory. I see from the knowledge records that they used to construct one pyramid over another. On an Earth site at Calakmul, rooms were discovered inside the pyramid, alongside finds that clearly depict UFOs and alien life forms. These were pyramids for healing and learning. These civilisations had monolith-type structures that harnessed energy, and were an amazing advancement for primitive humanity. Their people foretold events in human history, including the belief that the aliens would return. Since the Earth year 2012, there has been a massive energy shift towards these UFO beliefs and believing in other dimensions and energy realms. The Mayans predicted a massive change on Earth; it was not the end of Earth, as humanity believed, but it was the road to enlightenment. This was the start of a new era for humanity, destined to build steadily over time. These humanoids were from the advanced section of the humanoid races, bringing passed down ancient knowledge to enhance their culture. Remembering links to alien beings in ships, they were portrayed on their temple walls so humans could understand them. But as their lands were invaded by humans from other continents, disease broke down their infrastructure. Those that were left dispersed to try and survive elsewhere.

Now, from around 3000 BC to modern times on Earth, a race of beings was allowed to visit and explore the planet. We know them as Gorrombi, but we see Earth history simply called them the Greys. They were a small, pale grey race with oversized heads, no hair, large black eyes, no ears, small mouth, and pale grey skin. They also brought a similar race of beings with them who were taller, but similar in appearance, from the same solar system called Glapioni. They have not interfered in the DNA of humanity but have studied them closely. Evidence of them are on ancient cave walls – for example, old cave art in an area called Australia, depicts strange beings that resemble the Gorrombi 'Grey Alien.' These grey beings were known as Wandjina by the humans, which meant 'cloud spirits' and 'sky beings.' Also, in Chhattisgarh in an area called India, the local people depicted the small people who used to land from the sky on their cave dwelling walls. These two ascension alien races still visit the modern Earth, monitoring and trying to aid the Intergalactic Council in protecting the planet.

One of the next visiting off-world species I would like to tell you about is called Drygonmi; they came to Earth in fifth dimensional travelling spaceships, giving knowledge and wisdom to humanity. They are smaller than humankind, with a skin that you would describe as having a lizard-like texture, in human form. When they arrived on Earth they communicated telepathically with a civilisation called the Greeks. The Drygonmi come from a highly advanced, peaceful world, and travel the universe as explorers. Their influences are seen in Earth's history in the advancement of the Greek and Roman culture around 800 BC to 1453 AD, which spread across the Earth's lands and influenced other cultures. Earth's ancient history is full of records of ascension beings, so ask yourselves: where did the Greek and Roman gods come from? In Greek mythology you have tales of heroes, gods and demigods who walk among mortals, have great powers and great knowledge, and are capable of saving or destroying humanity. But these stories go beyond your Greek mythology; all over the world there are amazing tales of heroes, gods and demigods, and in all of those tales, these mythological creatures are described as having powers beyond human capabilities. I realise from the

Earth transcripts that the humanoids tried to understand these advanced beings the best they could, creating stories of them in the human form for the understanding of future generations.

Well, before your mind explodes with all this exciting knowledge it's time to take a break. I do have a great capacity for absorbing knowledge, but I understand as you read this you might appreciate some time out to reflect on all you are learning. I am meeting my mother tonight, as she is a guest of honour at an event recognising Diacuratian achievements. My father is picking us up so it's time for Freylen and me to find our finest garments and get ready.

I finish this transmission reflecting on a wonderful evening. I watched my mother give a passionate speech about her design work, creativity and the joy of teaching others. She received her work recognition with the humility that I love her for.

Life Journal – transmission 15
New Earth - The light beyond the horizon

Carrying on from the last transmission, Earth's history shows that during the time period of the Roman Empire the Intergalactic Council took the decision to not let any more ascension off-world species interact with humankind for a while. It was decided to allow highly ascended beings to incarnate to test the resilience of humanity against dark and the light. One example was a human whose Earth name was Jesus, in the Earth time period 4 BC – c. AD 33. Humanity of the time named him 'Son of God' as his earthly presence was so pure and different from the rest of humanity. His soul was from a plane of high ascension existence sent from the overseers through the Intergalactic Council. He had a link to spirit; a person with this gift is recognised in modern Earth language as a medium. Through his pure connection with his higher self he had healing hands and could even manifest simple things. The test with this human Jesus was to see how a warring civilisation would react to a radical force of change within their religions and societies. Other humans were born to be his followers, who were known in the scripts of Earth as disciples. This human led a simple life with no ego, always ensuring the best for others. His belief system created followers who threatened the power over figures in society, which eventually destroyed this great visionary.

After Jesus, the decision was again made that humanity was not ready for this light to be among them – although it must be said that humans then based a whole religion on the spark of light from this incarnated being brought to Earth. Even on modern day Earth, this man has his followers. Unfortunately, a lot of false detail was added to the manuscripts that followed this time, trying to recall or invent the events of this man's life. Over centuries much was distorted by ego and humanity, but many on modern day Earth still believe in the stories these writings tell. This high ascended being still works with Earth, showing his energy as the figure of human Jesus to try and bring hope and light to those in the dark. The overseers saw that he did actually have an impact after all, but not in the way they first thought he would. Where there is hope there can be light.

Other influences were introduced to Earth to try and bring enlightenment. One was Buddhism through a man named The Buddha (also known as Siddhartha Gautama) who lived in a land called India. His soul was brought to the Earth to be a spiritual teacher. He was a mendicant and had taken a vow to exist in poverty, relying on the kindness of others for survival. This belief allowed him to concentrate on his faith, preaching and serving his chosen society. He taught for around forty years, his teachings based on an insight into suffering and the end of suffering. From what I can see, Buddhism inspires humans to take responsibility for their own lives without moralising, which is achieved by understanding the effects of karma.

He taught his students to understand how humans can shape their future thoughts, words and actions, kindness bringing kindness – hate bringing hate. He also taught them that through meditation they could remove the negative memories already accumulated in the mind from past actions. He believed once the student could see how much suffering comes from simply not understanding its cause and effect, the human would naturally develop compassion. All of this of course helps the human form ascend while on the Earth plane. This religion is still part of the modern Earth world, helping to balance humanities existence.

As you know, these transmissions are to tell you about ascension beings who have visited Earth and influenced its history. If you know how and where to look, Earth's history is full of stories of visitors from other worlds; the evidence collected by humanity who witnessed these events is engraved in drawings on the walls of ancient civilisations, through to images captured by modern day humanity. The modern images are called unidentified flying objects – UFOs – by Earth dwellers. These are evidence of alien species – such as the Greys – who monitor and still occupy Earth to help aid in the experiments and humanity's ascension. But first of all, I will give you some ancient evidence that you can seek further knowledge on from the universal knowledge library or Earth's modern Internet and books.

Incarnated souls have also influenced humanity over the centuries; some of your greatest artists, philosophers, inspirers and inventors have had high spiritual connection from an unseen influence that has made them ahead of their time – Leonardo Da Vinci, Albert Einstein and Isaac Newton are just a few examples.

From Earth's history Freylen felt a great example was Leonardo Da Vinci, born in the Earth year of 1452; he was what you call a genius of his time. He was a painter, architect, inventor, and student of all things scientific. He was known best for his art, including two paintings that remain among the Earth world's most famous and admired, the Mona Lisa and the Last Supper. He was largely self-educated, and filled dozens of secret notebooks with inventions, observations and theories about pursuits from aeronautics to anatomy. The rest of the world was just starting to share knowledge in books, and most people found the concepts expressed in his notebooks were often difficult to interpret. As a result, though he was recognised in his time as a great artist, his contemporaries often did not fully appreciate his genius. Leonardo was capable of tapping into the universe's knowledge, and the combination of psychic intellect and imagination allowed him to create, at least on paper, such inventions as the bicycle, the helicopter and an aircraft based on the physiology and flying capability of a bat. But as you will know from reading your history, humanity was not ready for these inventions and theories; Leonardo was simply too advanced for his time – yet another test for humanity.

I would also like to mention Nostradamus, born in the Earth year 1503, one of your world's most famous authors of prophesies. He had quite a psychic, intuitive mind and tapped into universal knowledge, foreseeing future events with 'mind time travel'. Humanity's future is not set in stone, and although future scenarios can be seen by minds like his and ours, humanity can alter their futures with their actions. I only wish you could see what we see, so that this would become clear. A lot of Nostradamus's predictions regarding UFO encounters came true, and so will others. Take the time to read about him – you will be enlightened and fascinated by his life and predictions. But don't let this stress you, as futures can be altered by a shift to the light and living as one. Don't let your imagination run away with you. This was just a couple of samples I have read to inspire those who read these transcripts.

Art throughout Earths centuries depicts aliens and UFOs. Here are a few samples of what we have found; this is just the tip of the iceberg, so go off and investigate the examples given below and I am sure you will find it fascinating as I do. I feel from what I have read so far humanity needs to be more curious, to find out about their past and to secure their future. Look across your continents and societies new and ancient – every country has all of this evidence.

The Lolladoff Plate is a twelve-thousand-year-old stone dish that was found in Nepal. The pattern on the central disc spirals out from a sun, out of which there seems to appear a reptile, followed by a spaceship, followed by bacteria or atom designs, and then a reptile on the outer edge; at the centre of it all is a figure believed to represent an alien.

In Kimberly, Australia, 3000 BC humans recorded spirit beings in cave drawings; they were represented as giant humanoid figures, some measuring close to 23 feet tall, with grey alien-like eyes, cone-shaped heads, and no mouth or ears.

In the Sego Canyon 3000-5000 B.C., in an Earth area called state of Utah, USA, are cave paintings created by Anasazi and Fremont Native Indians. They show strange beings with exaggerated eyes, large craniums and physical size, similar to Australia's spirit beings. The Indians believed these drawings are the star people, the beings that came from the heavens to create people, and then returned from whence they came.

Pakal's tomb 683 A.D.: The design and engineering of this tomb are very similar to the Egyptian pyramids. The lid describes how Pakal's soul would return to the stars, from where he came. It shows the ruler seated upon the 'Monster of the Sun'. This term and the carving are clearly trying to communicate that Pakal took off from Earth in a spacecraft. The Mayans were using words they understood and images that aimed to represent what they saw. One can understand how a primitive Mayan would describe a rocket space ship blasting off as a monster. The blinding light of the engine exhaust as the rocket hurtled into space would look like the sun, hence the monster of the sun. Interesting, is it not?

In the year 776, a flying object was sighted during the siege of the Castle Sigiburg, in France. There are two illustrations of the incident on a twelfth-century manuscript, "Annales Laurissenses". Another UFO shape appears in the Notre-Dame Basilica Tapestry.

1327-Visoki Decani Monastery: The Crucifixion of Christ, as also seen in the Sventiskhoveli Cathedral, shows two flying objects in the upper left and right of the scene, piloted by beings that appear to be holding steering controls. Or are they futuristic time travellers, stopping by to see one of the major events in world history? All these are influenced by stories of visitors from outer space and other dimensions, with human interpretation reflected in the paintings.

The Annunciation with Saint Emidius, 1486: The Annunciation celebrates the announcement of Gabriel to Mary that she would conceive the Son of God. Humanity has always said that Mary got pregnant without conception; alien intervention has happened across human history, and this is one of your stories linked with this intervention. In the picture, alien saucers shoot light beams, which impregnated Earth women. It's interesting how these spaceships keep popping up in humanity's interpretations of the stories told in art.

Also remember Jesus's healing powers, his empathy and kindness; he descended from the heavens and was different to all other humans. Humanity was not ready for this new age man, as they had not developed far enough on their spiritual path. The powerful, greedy and scared humans were still in control and heavily outweighed those followers of Jesus who were starting to see the light back then. We are glad to say the balance on Earth today favours the change needed for you to ascend to where you need to be.

1561 - Battle of Nuremberg: The original woodcut prints by Hans Glaser, depicting the residents of Nuremberg, who saw what was described as an aerial battle of strange flying objects that flew with vapour trails and wielded spears at each other. This battle was followed by the appearance of a large black, triangular object that crashed outside the city. According to eyewitnesses, there were hundreds of spheres, cylinders and crosses engaged in the battle. The Intergalactic Council and alliances with ascension beings do sometimes face battles of light and dark. These stay mostly hidden in the dimensional layers around Earth and in the universe. The example given is one of the battles that slipped into the 3D energy matrix and the result is human eyes witnessed it.

In one of the oldest churches of Russia, in Svetitskhoveli, in Georgia, there is a fresco, dated from Earth's 17th century, where, on each side of the cross, one can distinguish two flying objects, inside each of which a face looks at the scene of the crucifixion of the man Jesus.

In 1710, a painting by well-known and Vatican-connected artist Aert de Gelder showed a UFO illuminating the baptism of Christ. There were other paintings showing Jesus Christ and UFOs, but when the French Revolution came this subject was beginning to be a threat to the Vatican (the people before this time were uneducated and not interested in art and paintings, except in the Renaissance period, when paintings featuring UFOs were particularly present). All artwork became subject to censorship, and any works that threatened the Vatican and its religious dogma were seized and banned.

In 1803, the Legend of Utsuro Bune (Hollow Ship) in Japan was recorded in drawings, the story of a star ship washed up on the shores of Japan. In this UFO was a young woman, depicted holding a box. My friends, please search out the rest of this story for your education on Earth.

In Salamankindca Cathedral Church, an image of what appears to be an astronaut is carved into the stone of a pillar. This work was started in the 1600s and finished in the 1800s.

As well as art, pottery figures have been found, depicting what look like men in space suits. Some have been found in Ecuador and in Kiev, dated to around 4,000 BC.

This is just a small sample of worldwide art evidence to show how in times past, humans believed that men who have gone before and walked amongst humans, were from the stars. I see over the last few Earth centuries that religious sects have suppressed these stories, but as they have shifted into the 20th century, all the old veils are being lifted. Humanity can no longer suppress this in the parts of the world that have freedom of speech. History also shows that once the whole Earth world sees these messages and all have freedom of speech, this will be the breakthrough that is needed for human ascension.

As well as works of art, I also want to reveal to you that there are ancient structures across the Earth that baffle humanity – the alien building blocks chosen to be left behind. The precision of them, the engineering way beyond human capabilities of those ancient times, suggest they were helped by alien civilisations over the centuries. Some are on land, and some are under the sea. A lot of them are built in alignment with the stars; these were guides for off-world beings, as well as footprints left for humanity to follow them home one day.

Again, I have selected a couple examples to inspire you to look further into your planet's history.

Tiwanaku is a pre-Columbian archaeological site in western Bolivia, South America. It was a city of an Atlantean empire that extended into your present-day Peru and Chile. The estimated 14,000-year old crumbled buildings still show geometrically perfect shapes which amaze humanity, as the pre-Columbian people that inhabited this region had no written language and still used stone and bronze tools, causing modern humans to question how they built these amazing structures. Even after centuries of outdoor erosion, you can still see the perfectly shaped stones, intricately routed patterns and perfectly drilled round holes of alien technology origins.

The Nazca Lines: Amongst the Nazca lines are giant shapes of monkeys and hummingbirds. Their purpose can't be explained readily, but you know how they were made: you figure out a shape and dig until you get to the different coloured rock. What is really interesting to us are the straight lines criss-crossing the plains. These stretch for up to 15 miles in some cases, but remain perfectly straight the entire way across, some as deep as 24 inches, and perfectly formed. Many humans believe this is aliens at work again, creating landing strips seen from space and other dimensions. Look at sun, star and mandalas, which are found in ancient messages for humans in Nazca and other parts of the world to this day.

I also reveal modern day crop circles in Earth's history – there are lots of circles and similar designs all around the world. Ascension beings have left symbols on Earth and landing guiding systems, along with messages for humanity to decipher. I see that many have not been discovered by humanity yet as they lay hidden under mountains, frozen lands or the Earth's oceans.

I could flood these transmissions with evidence from Earth that humanity has found, but I feel if we give a couple of samples this will ignite the curious minds amongst you to seek more. Seek the Earth book Utopia, which reveals much more. The times I have given of ascension beings occupation will reflect in the ancient history of humanity across all continents. By this I mean that humanity across Earth has interpreted events like Atlantis, through to the Greeks in art and written language. They have had to put it into the 3D energy context of their intellect and understanding.

To conclude this transmission Freylen wants to reveal the history of Chakra system on Earth. These are the central energy points that run through humans on Earth and were first introduced in the Atlantean experiments. The knowledge of this ancient spiritual connection and healing system stayed with some humans that survived and was used in many cultures, two being the ancient Hinduism and Buddhism healing systems. The overseers decided to reintroduce this healing system through an Earth man called Mikao Usui in Japan in the late 1800's creating the foundation of the practice of the Usui System of Natural Healing. They wished the Reiki healing system to spread into the modern western societies, to bring a stronger connection between humans and the ascended healing master guides that wished to work with humanity. This introduction of light divine healing has silently been successful in many humans guiding them on to the path of light and love.

Life Journal – transmission 16
New Earth - The light beyond the horizon

Phew, I had not realised how much there was for me to absorb from Earth's history! We are now ready to move into the planet's modern history and beyond to the year I incarnate into. But first of all, I wish to reveal Freylen's incarnation into the Earth period of the Egyptian times. This will give you another perspective of incarnation and ascension beings' influence on Earth.

Like mine, Freylen's existence is in a different time frame to Earth. It is hard to explain what might seem thousands of years ago on Earth can be a moment to her time frame existence. A modern human would find it difficult to understand how she can exist in this moment as you read, yet have also been incarnated a few thousand years ago of Earth's time. Let me explain: time can loop around through dimensions and we can enter a point of Earth's time frame to exist, as we understand it. In modern Earth's thinking, humans believe time is the progression of events from the past into the future and time moves only in one direction, so they think it's possible to move forward in time, but not backward. The human mind limits itself in this time restraint, worrying if they can get everything done in a 24-hour time period. This doubt and worry can restrict the flow of pure light, sound and colour frequency of their existence. When they take the worry away and just allow the moment to exist, they get a lot more done and will find they have extra time to relax. Take away the clocks and their existence would elevate because time would not matter to them, resulting in the creation of a higher ascension existence.

Freylen has given me a brief insight into her incarnated life for this transmission, when she lived on Earth in a city called Memphis. It was in the 27th century BC during the third dynasty of the Pharaoh *Djoser,* son of king Khasekhemwy and queen Nimaathap. Her human body was female, and she was the wife of the Pharaoh Djoser, named Hetephernebti. This was a time of high ascension beings incarnating, with some coming from the Earth names given to the Pleiades, Sirius, Ursa Major and Osiris regions of the stars. It was similar to the Atlantis time period when the Intergalactic Council wanted the humans to experience great awakening. The high ranking among the humans were chosen for this honour, with the human physical body and mind linking to the soul's purpose, and honouring the soul's home world.

Freylen explained how they built temples for the purpose of communication to the home worlds of incarnated souls, and for human healing and universal teachings. These temples were called pyramids; they were energy centres surrounded by the aid of waterways, light and sound which is multidimensional, which enhanced the power of the pyramids. The energy created in the pyramid's shape was unlike anything else on Earth. It harnessed the energy of space, light, sound and colour frequencies for the aid of healing and mind projection. Freylen described structures that varied in size, which were flat-sided, white polished pyramids with a vibrating golden glow from the pulsation energy created inside them. Priests and priestesses oversaw these temples, which allowed for enhancement of the human mind and physical body. The pyramids were linked up with walkways, waterways and lush garden areas for rest and peace. The large sacred pyramids were for the high-ranking humans with the high ascension souls, while the workers of the lands had smaller temples to use for their own worship of the sky gods and for healing.

The non-high-ranking Egyptian people had developed a belief system of a greater godlike power that controlled the movements of the constellations in the sky and the changing seasons on the Earth planet. They called the stars in these constellations 'the imperishable ones' linking with the celestial beliefs of eternal life. They tried to understand the power the king, queen and priests had over the lands and the people. They knew their essence went back to spirit, which they saw as the sky; this was their interpretation of the soul returning home. Freylen explained how they believed the human was made of various unseen forces, these being inner human essence, soul and ego. The ego was part of their human life and afterlife as they took forward the essence of the human life to the afterlife, the soul returning to the stars, the soul's home world or realm. I must say this showed a great understanding by these people of that time period, as all is correct.

Through the worship of this belief system and worshipping the sky gods it led them to linking the movement of the stars with points on Earth such as the North Pole. From this they had developed an Earth solar cycle of twelve parts and four seasons.

Freylen revealed to me from the universal knowledge library that they were a great civilisation and very advanced compared to a lot of the human Earth population. They rivalled the Greeks, Romans and Mayans in their understandings, thanks to the influence of ascension beings. Through these beings' teachings, the Egyptians became scientists, healers and great architects. A lot of their knowledge was translated into manuscripts by scribes; sadly, many have perished in the modern human world. In Freylen's time the court had a scribe called Seshat; her position was like a goddess of wisdom, recording knowledge, and she was a record keeper of events. We also noted this was also the era of inventing writing for communication.

I also saw images of highly decorated palaces, buildings and pyramids, rich with gold and rich colours of reds, blues, yellow and gems. The walls were decorated with paintings and hieroglyphics telling of their importance, beliefs for all to remember them by.

I could see that little evidence had been left of her life as a queen on Earth, apart from what's inscribed on her husband's tomb. I understand she had a very privileged life as she was born into high-ranking royalty and was a cousin of her husband. Throughout the history of ancient times many married siblings or cousins, as they believed it kept the royal bloodline purer. In fact, human history shows that close family offspring can be weaker and die younger. This was not something the ancient human scientists had knowledge of yet. In Freylen's time, a being known as Thoth, who was of high ascension, was an incarnated being. He again helped with manipulation of the human DNA, as they did in the Atlantean period, and he helped enhance their science. It is interesting to us both as we study this subject in the Earth's archives, as we see there were experiments within experiments.

As you can imagine, Freylen enjoyed a privileged incarnated life. She married Pharaoh Djoser at the age of fifteen. A woman in that time was married to a man as soon as she entered his house with the goods agreed upon beforehand. Her parents prearranged her marriage and reciprocal gifts were given from the groom's family to the bride's. She already knew Djoser and was not fearful of her marriage, in fact she embraced the union as it elevated her to Queen. She also explained he was a very intelligent human with a thirst for knowledge and love of architecture. After having three miscarriages and one stillborn child she eventually had a daughter called Inetkaes. There were no more children after her daughter, whom they worshipped. She reflected that her Earth husband ruled for twenty-one years and made many positive changes to the third ancient Egyptian dynasty. His legacy left knowledge for building, science and healing which then passed onto future generations.

Her human body died at the age of forty-one years; she contracted a fever that took her after four weeks of illness. Her husband had already passed back to the spirit realms, which affected her court position and had left her an outcast within the higher powers of the palace. Her daughter married a high-ranking court member and moved away from the city, so she felt quite isolated and Freylen the higher self, decided it was time to let go and leave the Earth plane.

Freylen reflected on this experience with me as changing her life's perspective. She has only had one experience of incarnation on Earth, and has now been selected for this time on Earth to try to elevate humanity's heavy energies again. Their process of incarnation is similar to ours, as they have also developed the ethereal multidimensional separation process. This allows a reflection of themselves to incarnate into human physical form and connect with all the body's senses and consciousness experiences. Freylen's physical form continued her life on her planet as this process was happening.

She would also have had a team of supporters for this process and guides that monitored the soul. She was always linked to her chosen incarnated life, tapping in when needed to guide and aid her reflection of self on its life's journey.

I end this transmission with news Freylen has just told me, that Siroian has just been appointed as a communications officer on Baltrexn's star ship. He told her he would transfer in a couple of light days. He will also use his negotiation skills in his new role as they come across new beings and civilisations. This means he will be more available to meet with Freylen. I knew there was a spark between them, and I look forward to seeing how this unfolds.

Life Journal – transmission 17
New Earth - The light beyond the horizon

I took a short break yesterday and spent it with my mother. She came to my dwelling to create new garments for me to wear. The materials we use are plant-based products created through a materialisation process. The texture can vary from what you would understand as a fine silk to a heavy wool. I had fun selecting the materials for the various garments I needed. Everything was sized on me from a light scanner that scans my body form and then shows options of the styles my mother has designed. It's like I am looking in a mirror and seeing myself in various designs and fabrics. When I have selected them, they are made to my mother's specifications while the materialisation light scanner moulds them to my physical body form. We invited Freylen to join us for dinner and mother offered to design some garments to her taste, which she gratefully accepted.

I continue with my Earth studies, reflecting that humanity had been left to evolve again on its own path with little outside influence from the beings that work in the light. Throughout the universe there is light; there is also darkness that includes beings that thrive on chaos in the universe. As with Atlantis, the dark energy finally ended the light experiments. There is always a silent battle going on of good conquering bad, and this shows up often in Earth's history in this next phase. As the Intergalactic Council had stepped back to let humanity evolve again naturally, the beings of the dark drew close to the planet to thrive on the negative energy the Earth wars fed into the universe.

Our research reveals the humans went into various stages of development over the next few centuries, which were named for example the Iron Age, the Middle Ages, and the Industrial Revolution. By the time of the Industrial Revolution, it was felt humanity needed to progress in its technology to help its evolution process. They could see that human minds had developed in their scientific knowledge and were ready to be influenced again by the Intergalactic Council and overseers of Earth. At this stage, the Intergalactic Council battled with the darker energies, forcing them to leave Earth's energy dimensions so the light could start to filter back in. I see from the planet's records that this forced the darker energies to become a bit more elusive in their behaviour, often infiltrating the light forces to cause havoc when they chose.

The overseers' plan was to further evolve human minds, spark new inventions and enhance their scientific contribution in the world – this became known as the Age of Science. The overseers had hoped the ancient technology and healing would have been embraced by the humans and would be built upon over the centuries. Sadly, it was lost in Earth's time and humanity digressed. So we see again the influence of light ascension beings bringing new ideas to the minds of those chosen for this task. I see the Industrial Revolution created machines, for example steam engines. These opened up world travel and led to mass manufacturing of useable items that were bought by humans. This shift brought about changes in the human culture as they moved from rural areas to big cities in order to work, and also had an impact on the environment. The Earth world also saw a big increase in population which, along with an increase in living standards, led to the start of the depletion of natural resources. They used steam, chemicals, and increased use of fossil fuels and this resulted in increased air and water pollution. I am not quite sure this was the push humanity had needed, as it was the start of the mass pollution of planet Earth.

The invention of electricity started another wave of evolution for power and technology. In our research of this subject we have found a good example to show you how the overseers influenced humanity. A man called Nikola Tesla was born to Earth with a star soul in the human year 1856, during a lightning storm at midnight. He was destined to connect to the universe's knowledge, led by his guides in the higher dimensional frequencies. He pursued ideas for wireless lighting and worldwide wireless electric power distribution in his high-voltage frequency exploration. Tesla had a car with an antenna that took the energy from an unseen source in the air and charged his batteries. He discovered that electrical power could be contained and harnessed, and this energy could be directed around the world not with cables, but by specially built masts strategically placed on Earth, creating wireless energy.

He discovered the zero-point energy field found everywhere in the space you exist in and the universe. He discovered that when, for example, you put direct current through a source, more energy came back – excess energy. This was recognised as an ocean of infinite energy – a phenomenon that could create an energy source for a vehicle that could move in any gravity, accelerating to a massless state. A name given to it was trans-dimensional – just think of our multidimensional existence and the portals of travel we have mentioned. Many beings use this type of travel to explore the universe. Some are able to exist in the multidimensional massless state and then return to physical form. On Earth, sadly, the power of bankers at the time meant that if you couldn't put it on a meter, they wouldn't invest in it. When we look at the dates of the twenty first century, all power, even natural solar and wind, was still calculated and charged using a meter. I can see from the Earth notes of this era that 99% percent of the population would have benefited from this clean energy, as well as Mother Earth. As it was, only one percent of the humans on Earth used their power for their own benefit to fill their bank accounts.

Tesla also worked on the possibility of wireless communication, but due to personal finances and lack of outside funding he struggled to succeed. Some thought he was a crackpot, especially as he believed he was getting downloads from a higher source. He revealed he saw flashing lights before the idea would come to him out of the blue, many of which were extending existing technology and raising it to the next level. He was not afraid to vocalise his experiences and of course, because of the restrictive way of thinking of the time he was not taken very seriously. The overseers made sure his ideas and work were recognised a few years after his death, as humanity's technology progressed. The overseers had hoped clean technology would be revealed to the industries working alongside the new inventions, but unfortunately the greed of the rich overseeing fossil fuels and oils prevailed. It saddens my heart to see this because if this energy source had been accepted at the time Mother Earth would not have been polluted by humanity. Freylen pointed out in the twenty first century, nearly a hundred years later, they were working on the theories of Tesla's findings and making great breakthroughs towards understanding clean energy.

On Diacurat we have a clean energy source with guidance from the original crystal left on our planet from the overseers. So I guess we were lucky, but we still had the free choice of whether to use it. It is just Earth's knowledge was chosen to be given to humanity in a different way, by channelling the information to those perceptive minds tuned to the universal frequency.

We see wars continued to rage on Earth. The two that are really interesting are what humans called the First and Second World Wars of Earth. This is when the overseers started to worry about the planet again as the negative energy of fear was so strong, other light beings in the universe were concerned about humans self-destructing.

The ancient records show many wars among humanity over thousands of years, some developing from failing societies to gain power over each other. These civilisations were developing and learning from their previous wars on how to improve strategy and gain the power and land they craved.

When we reflected on the Second World War in a time period of the twentieth century, we really noticed the difference in how humanity fought this war. As well as human power, it was the weapons of supremacy in the air, sea and land and the strategic methods they used that won the battles. We saw in the other wars that it was mainly the human soldiers who suffered the casualties, but in your last two world wars, especially the second, the civilians were greatly affected and displaced through fighting and the use of powerful new weapons.

What brought fear to the universe was the human discovery of the nuclear bomb, a destructive power that no being anywhere in the universe should have and use against others, but which humanity used twice in the Second World War. This led to the fear of Earth countries using their nuclear power as a control method to keep peace!

The knowledge of the nuclear bomb had not come from the overseers and there were dark forces influencing humanity's thinking. We see there is a race of beings called the Kaipul at this time, they are what we would call one of the darker alien species that do not wish to join the Intergalactic Council, but instead form a negative, thriving civilisation being led by Ego. They are a very advanced race in their technology, but their darker energies will never ascend much beyond where they are now. We also see from the records they have often tried to scuttle the overseers' plans; this seems to be a bit of a game to them in my view.

I cannot put into words how the overseers felt after what they witnessed on Earth. It was not just the bombs, but the persecution of individual races; one particular leader chose to eradicate a human population called the Jews, from his country of origin and those he invaded, with millions of lives displaced and murdered. Many of the light beings asked, what right has anybody got to persecute another, and say they are not worthy of living? We also see persecution amongst some races in humanity in their modern day, when humans see others lower than themselves and have no respect for them. You know, many light beings could have walked away at what they witnessed in the Second World War, but I see they kept the faith with humanity that one day they would learn from these terrible mistakes. They say you gain strength from hardship and life challenges and these war years definitely challenged the humans. We see after the First World War the Earth then was afflicted with a terrible disease named the Spanish flu. It lasted over two years and affected over 500,000 million humans, killing at least fifty million. This was a dark energy that disrupted Earth even more. The First World War took twenty million and the second world war over 75 million; we see there has never been such a large return of incarnated souls back to their home worlds up to this point.

I have to admit I feel quite emotional when I see these facts of Earth. This is what humanity does to each other when left on their own, which opened them up to the dark forces; they do not have the intelligence to see the bigger picture of what was happening. No wonder action was taken again to try to steer humanity back onto more of a spiritual light path. The purpose of the overseers and Intergalactic Council is to help humanity, and I realise this had got lost in their own processes of trying to learn and ascend from Earth's experiments.

Freylen reflected that the third-dimension energy matrix stopped the incarnated human soul remembering their Earth mission, and the soul within had to bring this forth to achieve their mission and ascension. But they were failing their missions due to our own pursuit of ascension, and forgetting the bigger picture, which was to bring peace, love and light to the planet. At this point of recognition, they asked across the universe for highly ascended light star beings in the fifth dimensions and beyond, to join them because they needed a new perspective on humanity and Earth. New alliances were formed and joined the Earth mission as spirit within souls and guides. They were asked to gather information from their missions that would help aid humanity to ascend.

I wondered why the overseers did not stop these wars, as they knew what was happening from afar; when I say Earth is left alone it is still observed. But we see from the light side that the wars were allowed to develop and happen as there was always that hope humanity would ascend on their own to stop this chain of events. Souls are contracted for the possible timeline of Earth, as there can be many, but this destructive darkness can be altered with a mass awakening of the spiritual path.

Something my people learnt many hyons ago is to always pursue a peaceful solution to all things. Saying this, the records do show among humanity, that in a time of crisis a new positive bond can form. This develops when humans want to stop the harm people are doing to each other, and humans will help each other in times of need when faced with adversity, no matter what their background or race. We found the latter experience made all equal, which gave hope for humanity. Because of this, the light ascension beings decided to carry on with Earth, seeing good could prevail over the darkness.

The archives show that after the war, when all the horrors were revealed and the full extent of the persecution of individual races was understood, most of humanity was in disbelief and shock. After deep discussion on this subject, Freylen and I felt that when humanity is left to its own devices, it takes a crisis for humans to see the bad in others and to bring out the good. But we see that human beings do not learn from this; it will take the ones with power over them – the leaders – to awaken and lead the way for peace to make a real difference. The humans under these 'Power over leaders' for centuries needed to speak out about what they wanted for humanity, such as peace; humans would be surprised by how many of them want peace and an environmentally safe world, but are afraid of persecution and their voices being heard.

Up to this point we see the humans were being guided from the incarnated soul, hoping they would feel this inner connection and change their behaviour. With this new understanding it would lead to the spiritual way, but this was not working. There were yet again darker influences guiding the humans unknowingly - remember the end of Atlantis and the Kaiplu. There are beings that do not wish Earth well and thrive on mayhem and war. They can influence the energy of Earth in this direction, taking advantage when the Intergalactic Council backs off from the Earth to just observe, then they make their moves. I see many battles in the dimensions have been fought with these beings and the Intergalactic Council win, with humanity having no idea this was taking place.

Another battle of dark against light was won and this led to a new phase of experiments to help bring an awakening to humanity. This was the process of bringing in humans with a higher-light level frequency adjustment to their DNA, creating this when the reflective self of the chosen beings joined with them as the soul within. These new-borns went to Earth as Indigo, Crystal, Rainbow or Star children and they are all programmed with a greater purpose on Earth. They were put in positions around the planet and their DNA was waiting to be activated when the time was right, before, during or after the awakening. When activated they would remember their light purpose, which was mainly to bring in the spiritual way of being and gather information of how to bring peace and unity to humanity. These people became holistic healers, mediums or humans living in a pure light and love existence by helping others; they were givers to humanity and the animal kingdom. I won't go into great detail about them, as there are lots of transmissions or Earth books that explain their purpose for Earth for your understanding.

These children grew up and became peace campaigners

throughout the world in the nineteen sixties and seventies timeline, often depicted as the hippy generation for equal unity living. The archive shows this created a higher energy frequency on Earth and helped the world move forward in a kindlier way of being. At this point, the selected high ascension beings also became more involved again, monitoring the Earth and her progress, hence the high number of unexplained objects known as UFOs that now again appear in Earth's history records.

On this new phase of experiment, the good news was that these children as they grew were remembering their mission and connecting to their multidimensional spiritual energy. But at the same time some of the children struggled with their high frequency energy in the heavy three dimensions. This made them appear to have behavioural problems and humanity did not know about them and their higher purpose. So often these children were segregated as learners with difficulties, and classed differently to the other Earth children. Sadly, we see that often drugs were used to change their behaviour, which alerted the Intergalactic Council to this problem. By the twenty first century they had started to reprogram and improve the new chosen children's energies. These children were to bring enlightenment to the spiritual movement, and we see their energies did adapt better to the heavier energies of Earth. This continued to be a battle into the twenty second century due to Earth's many frequency changes.

While this new spiritual movement on Earth was picking up pace there were further ground-breaking inventions. Although they seem primitive to us, for humanity it was another phase of their evolution. The highlights of this progress that show in their history were communications, phones and radios, and the enhancement of electric goods such as televisions. There was also advancement of electric goods for the home such as microwaves, fridges and recording machines. We feel the technology given to them such as computers was a massive leap, leading to the Earth knowledge being on the Internet for all to access. From the nineteen fifties they were led to space exploration, but the Intergalactic Council wanted to make sure this progress was slow because of humanity's weapons and violent nature. They allowed rockets as far as the moon, satellites and space probes which revealed to humanity more about the planets of their solar system. It was hoped this primitive space knowledge would allow humanity to see there is so much more than humans and planet Earth. They thought it would lead to expansion of their minds to all the vast possibilities the universe could offer, helping them expand beyond their 3D energy restraints. In the Earth's modern time period this has not happened, so the Intergalactic Council has made sure the Earth's visitors' ascension beings space crafts and stations in the solar system have mostly remained hidden from these probes and the human eye. It has been hard for them to remain hidden round Earth all the time and new digital technology has captured crafts and energy images when they have been off guard. But we see from the records there was an understanding there was a balance of keeping humanity's awareness of us all and not scaring them, which would cause human societies to break down. The Intergalactic Council waited for the day they could reveal themselves to humanity.

Life Journal – transmission 18
New Earth - The light beyond the horizon'

Before I start my next session of learning about Earth's history, I am enjoying some me time. I am in my favourite chair sitting with Peagal on my lap, with my face reflecting a huge smile as I look out across the beautiful lake. As I gently stroke Peagal he leans against my hand enjoying this attention, he makes a deep rumbling sound as his colours change to his surroundings, which reflects my clothes, nature, sky and the lake. The reason for my happiness is when Freylen and myself were studying two light days ago, Baltrexn and Siroian arrived unexpectedly. Baltrexn had managed to keep it a surprise, even blocked from our mind-to-mind connection. My face must have been a picture of happiness and I thought Freylen looked a bit shy but also very pleased to see Siroian.

Their ship had to come back to Diacurat as there were some important dignitaries that needed to be transported to the space station for an urgent intergalactic meeting there. They were here for two light days before taking them back to their home planet. The dignitaries were Geltarian beings, who live in a liquid substance on their planet and do not travel well through the portholes of space. The Geltarian need to be surrounded by this liquid energy life force to survive and it becomes unstable in the portholes. The scientists of the galactic nation's worlds have been working with them on this in the hope that one day stable travel could be achieved for them. There were also other species that would benefit from this new technology when created.

Baltrexn showed me images of them; they are a beautiful species, and their skin reflects the world around them, reminding me a bit of Peagal. They have small heads, a slim upper torso, arms with delicate webbed fingers, but no legs. Their lower body reminded me of a long, delicate fish, which they used to propel themselves through their environment. They were a highly intelligent telepathic race yet had kept their existence fairly simple. They now have the capacity to leave their planet and explore only their own solar system, and had not gone beyond until now. They had had contact with our people as we visited their solar system and through this the Intergalactic Council had recognised them as a loving, considerate and intelligent race. They felt they could bring this beautiful energy balance to the Intergalactic Council and it would help to serve their cause of enlightenment. Baltrexn's ship had built them a large eco apartment to cater for them as they travelled through space. As long as this was kept stable there would be no issues with their life force and survival.

Well, with these two handsome beings' appearance, we decided to make the most of their visit, and thought it would be nice to show Siroian and Freylen some of our planet and its beauty. So we headed off to an area called Pycyran, a mountainous area of lakes with beaches of purple sand. Since the weather system Zelicann left our planet, more leisure dwellings have been built on the surface for our pleasure. A resort had been built at Pycyran, solely created for relaxation and meditation purposes. We had a large dwelling that catered for all our needs for two days. It was such a relaxing experience, we enjoyed swimming in the lakes, and watching the beautiful life that inhabits these areas. In the dark hours we sat under the stars, talking about our lives and experiences. Siroian was quite interested in the incarnation experience I was going to undertake and Freylen entranced him with her experience of her life on Earth. He had never had this experience himself; as yet, his life purpose had not steered him in that direction.

The two days went by far too quickly, leaving Freylen and me at a bit of a loss when they left. There was now a stronger bond between Freylen and Siroian, both having a renewed sparkle in their eyes. Baltrexn told me later to say he believed Siroian was quite infatuated with Freylen, and he had commented she was different to any other Pleiadean he had met. We both felt quite excited for them.

Rather than dwell on them leaving us again we refocused on our work and threw ourselves back into our Earth studies. Our next phase of the planet's history is the end of the twentieth century and the beginning of the twenty-first – a date I see the overseers choose again to try and help shift humanity's energy into a more positive time frame. The build-up to the start of this change was in the year 1999 as they approached the timeline of the millennium year 2000. Humanity remained unsatisfied with itself and they put faith in the start of a new century. We see in the records that this really helped to raise the Earth's energy for a few months. There was again a wave of spiritual awakening and on the back of this new energy, more and more star children were born to Earth. This was all with the continued hope that humanity would stop mistreating each other and the Mother Earth. But sadly, we see humanity continued on a downward spiral leading the overseers and the Intergalactic Council to review the future of Earth and the human race. If they carried on this course of self-destruction, both could perish.

Life Journal – transmission 19
New Earth - The light beyond the horizon

This light day I met again with Havrium from my incarnation team at the mind and body travel institute and Freylen attended with me. Havrium wanted to see how we were progressing with our Earth studies and if we had any more questions to ask him. We explained we found the diversities of Earth's history very interesting. Also, we would soon be finished as we were now entering the last two hundred years of history before my chosen incarnation year.

My first three guides that would be with me had now been confirmed as Freylen, Oucustion and Pactsaceon. Both Freylen and I were delighted that she was going to be part of my Earth journey; her guidance would be invaluable to the experience. Oucustion and Pactsaceon were introduced to me at the meeting.

Oucustion is a fellow Diacuratian but I had not met him before. He has been a guide many times for our people and also had experience of the Earth journey as an incarnated soul. I was very excited by his presence; he was a mature member of our society with much wisdom and valuable insight which could only enhance my incarnation experience. He would be my main guide or, as Earth beings came to call them, gatekeepers. He would be connected with me at the moment my reflection of self (soul) incarnates and through the whole journey until the soul returns home to become whole again with my energies. Oucustion's daylight job was working with our natural energy source from our light star. I suppose in Earth language terms, he is like an engineer, making sure all is safe and clean with the technology we use. We have a crystal energy source that absorbs the light star's energy and can be tapped into with set frequencies and intention of thought to trigger the clean energy power source. We also use an energy source of tapping into the hidden energies that surround us and our planet, and spaceships are also powered by these two energy sources. Oucustion was familiar already with Earth's history for his guide role and said we could contact him if we had questions.

Pactsaceon was an Arcturian from the planet Uyomini from the Arcturia star system, sometimes known as the blue planet. He was a very handsome being with a rich blue skin, elongated head, and moved with such grace that he seemed to float. He had been involved in the Arcturian incarnation program for a very long time and had also had the earth soul experience. He explained the people of his race were naturally critical thinkers, analysts, healers for the emotional base line of energy, creative, and travellers. They have the choice of physical and multidimensional form, which lends well to the incarnation process. He explained they love to help individuals to whole civilisations on their ascension transcendent path. He told us he had not been to his home world for a long time as he travelled the expanse of the universe answering calls for his experience and assistance. Pactsaceon had been recommended to our sacred light council by the Intergalactic Council, saying that there is no ego with this being, just a modest way of saying things as they are fact. I must say Freylen and myself look forward to getting to know Oucustion and Pactsaceon as this adventure comes nearer.

And on this thought we all decided, as we had some free time, to have lunch at Fancasapian Gardens. They had a beautiful dining space and the gardens held many rare plant life species.

A lot of these had to be kept in their own biospheres because of their unusual habitats. There were also some very interesting specimens from other worlds. One that fascinated me had a large, flat upright flower head that caught living insects and digested them, perhaps a bit ugly, but I had never seen anything quite like it. Many of the plant species would respond to your touch and I felt they were trying to communicate with us. I know it is possible for us to set our frequencies to theirs, but botanical scientists really wanted the plants to interact with us at a low level, so we did not affect their energies too much, especially the off-world species. These scientists studied them but limited their contact, as all ascension species' feelings have to be considered, including animal and plant life. It was very important all the plants were happy in their own environments as some were away from their original home worlds.

We agreed to set a date to meet at the mind and body travel institute to discuss the processes and get to know each other better. Havrium set the daylight meeting dates and we all said farewell, promising to keep mind linked for our progress updates.

We had no time to waste so Freylen and myself went back at our Earth studies. We were now studying the first twenty years of the twenty first century. There were many advancements in the Earth's technology and here are a few for you to consider from the Earth's archives:

Artificial Intelligence (AI)
The Electric Car
Smart phones
AbioCor Artificial Heart
3D printing of all forms

Augmented reality graphics
Gene and DNA editing
Miniaturisation of computer technology
Virtual assistant technology
Tokenisation
Touch screen glass
Advancements in medicine
Quantum physics
Photonic Crystals and Light Localisation
Harnessing Zero-Point Energy

These are some of the key advancements we found; if you wish to extend your education further, see the transmissions for Earth on the twenty first century, or if you are on Earth, in books and the Internet.

There was also a lot that lay hidden from humanity from the powers who ran Earth's societies. Crystal technology existed in a computer storage form, energy containment and force fields, while top scientists also knew about energy frequency travel portals. There was a secret space program based on UFO technology; this had not progressed too far as the overseers held back their advancements. Many so-called cures, for example for cancer, killed the patients before it cured them. They explored telepathic mind control and they knew mind over body could cure many illnesses physically and mentally as well as natural earth remedies. They knew that at a lot of human illnesses came from the pollution, poisoned by the lands, food, air, water supplies and stress of modern day life on Earth. That they had added chemicals to water supplies that tried to clear the pollutants and affected human cell structure. Vaccines had been invented with markers in them for tracking and I could go on. I know this because in the recorded history of all civilisations nothing is hidden, all reasons for their being is recorded; all acts of light and dark.

I was quite shocked by how much was hidden from humanity by the one percent that could change the world for the better, so that humans could live free, healthy lives and each fulfil their potential. Instead, they had nearly all developed into indoctrinated, heavy, three-dimensional controlled societies that thought they were free-thinking. All societies have boundaries in some form as we do, but to survive, humanity needed to exist in honesty, kindness and unification, with respect for all life forms. It was obvious that this time period was run on materialistic wealth and greed, without concern for the damage it did to the environment of Earth and humanity.

All of this was leading to Mother Earth being poisoned from air, ground and sea, and she was slowly suffocating. I see there were souls put in place to break down the powers of control and try to make humanity see that what they were doing was wrong. An example I found was something called the Green Peace movement, with both elderly and young individuals speaking out about pollution and gaining momentum with followers who also spoke their words. Governments around the world were lobbied to stop pollution and save the environment, but many ignored it or by the time they listened it was too late. By the year 2020 the Earth was warming to a point of critical no return with ice caps and glaciers melting and severe weather changes. These had slowly been getting worse since the late 1990s. Earth had always had occasional odd weather patterns, but I see these were now yearly.

Pollution had stopped the natural evolution of Earth and she was struggling to survive and sustain humanity. Her dimensional energies were now vibrating at inconsistent frequencies, causing a chain reaction that created severe storms, earthquakes and very prolonged dry and hot or wet weather conditions. The natural habitats of many animal species were destroyed, and many became extinct. The Earth poles had shifted slightly by this point too, something else that was not reported in the mainstream news of the time. There were far too many humans for the world to sustain and again, I could go on. It was at this latter point of the lead up to 2020 that the overseers decided to step in again. The Earth needed an awakening event to open the human's eyes to what they were doing. Wars were not an option, as they would destroy the planet further and humanity did not learn from them as past history showed. After many meetings with the overseers and the Intergalactic Council they decided on a viral pandemic.

This would be triggered by what was called a virus; it would be a new virus that would manifest from a human mucus cell structure with many facets to it. It would be passed on through breath and touch and manifest in the blood, affecting the whole body. It would be designed to mainly take the weak and old of society. The virus would have an evolving structure; when it infected certain healthy humans with the preordained DNA trigger it would mutate and make them extremely ill and in some cases, would be fatal. The reason for this was to create a fear of the virus. This DNA trigger lays dormant unless the overseers need to trigger it, an example of this was seen at the end of the Atlantis experiment. Many Atlanteans were asked at soul level if they wish to return to their home worlds or live out their Earth life in the aftermath of the Atlantis cities' destruction. For those that chose to leave the planet early, various ways were triggered for their physical body to die through the DNA trigger.

This new virus took many souls back to their home worlds and the overseers had asked the higher selves if it was acceptable for them to leave the Earth in this wave of deaths. Permission was required, as they had entered into the soul contract with many lessons to learn. They had a lifeline structure and family that was preordained, but the higher self can leave earlier if necessary, as for example for the awakening on Earth to aid humanity. As the higher source of divine power, the overseers can manipulate all souls' lifelines left behind in the event of an early exit. The souls left on Earth can carry on their ordained path and the higher self can also decide if there is a change of plan for new learning path while still in the human body.

With this virus, many light being observers were also sent to influence minds and create fear in the minds of humanity, because the overseers wanted the Earth to slow down, and humanity to stop and revaluate themselves. So a situation was created where humans were asked to lock down in their dwellings and not mix with family and friends or go to work. But they ensured there was a human support network in place for survival for food, fuel and medical care, so society did not break down.

I asked Oucustion for his thoughts on this time period and this was his response to me: When this event was triggered on Earth, humanity had lots of theories to explain what was happening to the world around them. As we have already revealed, humanity has been influenced by ascensions beings for thousands of years and still is. As you know, these beings vary from physical form to ethereal multidimensional beings. For the human language, the word experiment has been used for their understanding. These experiments over Earth's timeline were creating humans and influencing them to try to create a sustainable utopia. I remind you that Earth has had ascension being visitors for millions of years, but no evidence has survived. Now go back 12,000 years in Earth's history, when humans were starting to record the ascension beings on cave walls and gods and deities were created from their influence. Religions were sparked from the feeling of a force unseen, but felt in the heart from incarnated souls within the humans.

The influence of these beings on Earth was mixed, as not all worked in the light. A long time ago, the overseers of the universe created the Intergalactic Council to pull together all the ascension beings working in the light. With their telepathic skills and technology, they sought to bring their light across the universe, helping others to ascend into the light and love way of existing. As you know, Earth was chosen for this purpose.

Think of these ascension beings in the light as friends of humanity. Humans had free will to a point; there were gaps in the overseers' influence when we left humanity alone and as Earth history shows darkness came, and with that, wars. So, at various times when humanity needed a push back into the light, they telepathically influenced their minds, trying to guide them onto the path of ascension. This ascension path helps humans to be influenced to love each other, bringing kindness to humanity and the Mother Earth. They could heal themselves and each other if they reached the understanding of four to five-dimensional clarity.

At the end of Earth's second world war, the overseers felt they were failing humanity and Mother Earth, so they called upon many ascension beings from the light across the universe to come and help them. Through these new alliances, they influenced technology, and the progression of humanity and their aim was the hope they would develop clean energy and have a global unity with no more wars, just peace. As you know this happened, but we struggled against the dark energy of greed of those that seek the power of control and humanity exploiting each other. For example, clean technology exists but does not fill the pockets of the rich; it should be free to all, but it remained at this time hidden from the Earth societies by the power over darker energies. The overseers sometimes had to accept these darker influences were more powerful when the light forces were not so influential on Earth. They always hoped the humans would be strong enough to eradicate this on their own with a soul and higher self-connection support network. The overseers and Intergalactic Council fought battles in various dimensional existences to eradicate the dark energy beings influencing the Earth.

The overseers brought their message through ascension beings to Earth's governments through physical interaction and mind connection, but this stayed behind closed doors and was misused by those who had the privilege of meeting these beings. The overseers then decided to bring the message of change to the people through trance mediums, channellers and the souls placed that had agreed to be triggered to spread their purpose of new hope into humanity. With this now finally in place by late 2019, the overseers started to see a shift in human energies.

The overseers then had to plan a strategy to build on this progress. They needed to slow the world down and give humans time to reflect and support each other in times of crisis, to create a situation that would influence the minds of the scientists and leaders to talk to each other. For hidden agendas to be revealed to the public domain of human society, so humanity could question their reality. This was also a time for all spiritual people to start using their telepathic mind power to send healing, so they understood the power of telepathic connection. But the main reason was to help heal Mother Earth so she and humanity could survive.

This virus infection was no worse than anything else that had yet been created on Earth, but was designed to open minds rather than destroy humanity. As with any illness it would take the weak, but the souls accepted this to help humanity. Humans all have a unique single purpose that many of them are unaware of, until the overseers trigger their purpose.

As the virus took hold round the Earth the overseers could see the shift in humanity's thinking and many things were being revealed to them through changes being imposed on the population. Money was not as important, materialistic items could be lived without, and what they had was valued more. Families were divided due to quarantine restrictions and this helped humanity appreciate each other and the freedom they once had. This period of time unleashed pent up anger, for example over how humanity treated each other because of the colour of their skin. The Earth word racism was used and this human way of thinking I see went back centuries. The world went into deep financial recession that caused further dark ways of existence with frustration and riots. The shift of the old energy to the new brought this unrest for many but also created positive change. People started to question how they lived and were drawn to the smaller community concept. Images started to emerge of Mother Earth healing, seas clearing, animals coming back to old habitats, because humans were not actively trampling Earth, and this meant less pollution.

The overseers observed firstly those humans that had to isolate in their dwellings, finding solitude, solidarity, and the challenge of mind and self-awakening through this process. Secondly, those humans who were named as being on the front line, which were the key workers and the sick. These humans found challenges of mind and body, solidarity, some solitude, new inner strength and self-awakening.

Humans separated off into two halves, those who supported and helped each other, and those who were selfish and used this humanity-awakening event to seize power over others for materialistic gain. These humans fall into both of society's first two groups. No matter their religion or creed they had to dig deep inside to find strength to get through this.

Many humans experienced isolation and loneliness at the end of their lives, but their soul level was always supported during this process and the chosen guides kept the soul safe on its transition home. The humans that were already awakened used the awakening time space to rediscover themselves and their true ordained Earth's path. They had to dig deeper than they ever had before to reach their soul level and life's purpose. They learned about trusting their intuition, which comes from the soul level of the human experience.

It was observed that many humans could not understand this virus, as the number ill and dying were lower than that, say, of a flu epidemic. All sorts of conspiracy theories circulated, being fed by the darker fear based energies. It did not matter if this was a human built contagion, or Earth's reaction to technology and pollution, it was triggered by an ordained higher power source to try and help humanity. The decision was made on this Earth's timeline based on previous Earth events that led to this point of desperation. The overseers and Intergalactic Council had really hoped it would not come to this but stepped into bring a needed awakening to humanity, so to give Mother Earth a chance to heal and reset her energies. Further strains of the virus and other biological threats were triggered to bring more awakening up to the Earth year 2030. These were all arranged as it was time for humanity to slow down and reflect on their very existence and what they were doing to Mother Earth and each other.

I have to thank Oucustion for his insight into this period of Mother Earth's history. I also see from the recorded history of Earth that the awakening caused two frequency paths on the planet, one being the old Earth pattern and the other, the 'New Earth'. The way they lived their normal lives changed in the period of lock down of the virus and those who awakened started living on the new Earth frequency. Many on this new frequency understood that they had mistreated humans, animals, and Mother Earth was more important than a materialistic existence. This shift of energy opened up the portals for truth. Those in the darker energy positions of control and power on Earth, just over one percent of humans, were starting to be exposed for who they really were. Some of them experienced fortunes slipping through their hands, having a real reality check. It also came to light that a leader of the time of the western world was actually in place to reveal many things that were sealed behind closed doors. A man of great wealth, who bought his power but had a purpose on Earth others did not see. This was the start of a time of great change.

Life Journal – transmission 20
New Earth - The light beyond the horizon

As we explore beyond the period of the new awakening, I see the new Earth frequency grew in strength as humanity learned the value of life from more events that happened on the planet's timeline. Through the light workers and scientists, it became apparent that humans had a telepathic link and when they worked simultaneously with their mind powers as one, they could harness this energy for great things such as individual and world healing.

They realised they were capable of focused thought, especially if a number of people trained in mind control worked together; they could manipulate physical objects as we can and the ascended ancients on Earth did. The governments were also aware of how many light workers were telepathically linking with ascension beings and receiving messages and downloads of knowledge. This unsettled the human observers of humanity; they had to hold back taking any action against them, as it would mean thousands of humans would have to disappear, in fact the whole of the light worker spiritual movement of that time. So they decided to observe through social media and technology and try to learn from this contact from many ascension beings.

As the awakening grew in strength over the years the humans ascended into the fifth-dimensional understanding, developing their higher minds and concentrating on creation for the highest good of all. There was an exponential shift in their understanding and use of their powers. While this light way of being became more of the norm it was vital to stop the dark, heavy energy using this for mind control over others. The old

Earth frequency still existed, and it ran alongside the 'New Earth' frequency for the next 50 years.

The next ten years after 2020 brought many revelations to humanity, especially when the truths of alien ascension beings making contact was revealed to them; this created shock waves, especially within the religions on Earth. This gave rise to more humans questioning centuries of deep-set beliefs and their faith in God was challenged. Many started to understand the spiritual way of life could be for all, no matter what creed or religion. Religions stopped fighting for supremacy and slowly started to respect each other more. The spiritual movement really was growing across the world. This was achieved by the new awakening energy breaking down the barriers of creeds and religions to work in unity of oneness. The new energy started to close the gap between observer and the observed, breaking down the old barriers and creating a new spiritual beginning of change around the world.

Spiritualism in the universe is not a religion; it is a way of existence in the light. The essence of this is respecting each other's beliefs and uniqueness but all living by true spiritual values:

Kindness

Honesty

Love

Compassion

Gratitude

Supporting others

Friendship

Non-judgment

Selflessness

Empathy

These values are what we on Diacurat live by; we know from experience that this spiritual way of life brings a massive change to the individual and any world as a whole. For humanity, it meant a gradual change in perspective on many things, allowing a portal for truth to be opened. They began to show new respect for Mother Earth, and many started to see she needed to heal so all could feel a new truth frequency of the vibration of love.

In this time period, Mother Earth had reached saturation point with pollution, while the natural fuel resources were being exhausted. The awakening had started to bring greater awareness to humanity of what they were doing to their planet, but there were over seven billion people to reach and it would not be a fast process. The awakening did not stop Mother Earth's reaction to the pollution, but the new awakened human minds were able to send healing that helped. Mother Earth's reaction would have been a lot worse with more disasters if this had not happened. You must realise that every time a human sent healing via their healing guides, other ascension beings and observers joined them to magnify the energy. Humans learnt that this remote healing in groups was more powerful and became more widely used by awakened human light workers. Meditation started to come to the forefront of everyday life, which enhanced this process. This is how we developed our multidimensional powers on Diacurat, working with this basic remote healing system. But this did take many, many hyons and we are still learning and growing in this way of existence.

During the awakening in 2020 when the world slowed down and pollution levels dropped, the damaged ozone layer started to heal. This was a big trigger point for humans, realising how much they were damaging the planet. The conservationists finally had proof that could not be denied by the governments. Mother Earth's reaction to the pollution had already been triggered and there were more severe natural disasters to come. There were earthquakes in the eastern and western world; on the American continent there were tsunamis off their coastlines and a volcano erupting for months stopped flights. There were more severe droughts and monsoons around the world, causing many more humans to be displaced through climate change, while some populations decreased with the natural disasters. I was wondering why the overseers could not stop this, but realised the 2020 awakening unleashed a tide of events that had to happen to build on this new Earth frequency. It was all about shifting Earth and humanity into the light. Eventually the planet did settle, and the new Earth frequency just kept growing in strength.

Freylen pointed out how this awakening triggered new positive energy towards conservation on Earth of beauty spots and saving wildlife threatened by human hunting, pollution and climate change disasters. There were some already in place, but this came to the forefront of what was valued in life and governments got on board to support them. By the end of these ten years, all governments had admitted climate change existed and had started to plan the future of humanity around it.

As the Earth time approached 2030 the world economy had collapsed, mainly as the awakening had created a stall in business; this caused huge corporations to stop trading, with a massive knock-on effect on all businesses worldwide. The world leaders decided to reboot the world economy with a global currency for all countries. The thought behind this was that as world trade was changing, a single currency would take away the individual currency risk for traders. It would mean that world traders would no longer have to hedge their positions in fear of currency fluctuations. When the global currency was introduced the businesses of the world started to feel safe again, and price competition started to stop, bringing fair prices for all and increased trade. Developing countries also benefited considerably, with the introduction of a stable currency, which formed a base for future economic development and helped to stop poverty. The style of the way humans worked had also changed, mainly from the on and off lock down periods in 2020 to 2022. Many started to work from home, multi corporate companies let their offices go and started this way of working. By 2030 this was common practice and the small business and home business thrived.

By 2037 the Earth's climate had started to settle and the world's peoples were populating old and new habitats, creating smaller living communities. The awakening period brought scientists and light workers together for a new understanding of mind healing with technology. The old power over leaders had toppled by this time and humans now saw a new energy light of coexisting, together with new leaders who were working within the new Earth frequency. Part of this was letting go of blame and learning to reboot themselves and their way of thinking.

With the high pollution of the world now at the forefront of global leaders' concerns, they started to look more seriously at how humans travelled, and how to stop further pollution and the fuel crisis. Electric cars had become the norm for many families, which was a step forward. Also, solar powered vehicles were being developed with self-energising technology. You see, even though electric cars helped, there was still the underlying pollution that came from the energy plants that made the electric source. Conversations about clean energy were now on the world leaders' agenda and seen as a priority. The decision also had been made to shut all nuclear plants when clean energy was established throughout the world.

By 2040 the overseers saw hope for humanity and allowed the frequencies of the universal knowledge be filtered through to the minds of those ready to receive. One of these was crystal technology to hold information, which had developed well beyond the use of silicone chips in computers. Humans were now ready for more enlightenment, as it was felt they would not abuse this new technology. Crystals were being programmed once more to help humanity, as the ascension ancient ones once had. They could hold information, be a light/heat source and be used for healing powers. The souls of the ancient ones had already reincarnated so they could help with this process. The crystals could retain so much information and humans also learned how to use them to heat their homes, give light, and channel healing.

Another step forward was medicine; in the last ten years medicine had altered for physical and mind treatments. The dominant pharmaceutical companies no longer had the upper hand as many humans now recognised holistic medicine and healing. Natural medicine doctors became the norm, working alongside the doctors of the old Earth energy way of understanding.

A greater understanding of light, sound and colour spectrum frequencies and mindset was used to heal human bodies. The new way of medicine was about balancing people's energy points like chakras and using natural herbs and natural products. Meditation and mindfulness were now part of most human's daily lives, making sure all children were taught this from an early age. They helped everyone maintain the maximum balanced flow of energy in their bodies.

Other advancements in this time period leading up to 2050, included the use of plant products to replace plastics. Clean technology and energy harnessed from water, wind and the star sun became the norm, eventually being supplied free to the world. The deforestation of the planet had stopped as new sustainable bio-gradable materials had been created. Everything that was no longer of use to humans was recycled and landfill became a thing of the past. These next thirty years after 2020 were the start of a great shift for humanity.

Freylen was quite absorbed in this time period, as she found it very interesting. She observed that part of the healing processes sought by the overseers was for humanity to feel the struggle of letting go the human ego, having power over each other, materialistic jealousy and the selfish existence of culture hate. When humanity realised this was no longer serving their survival, then the awakening for them all really began. The only way they could make humanity see this was to slow down their world. When civilisations all live at a fast pace, they are blind to the obvious reality of self-destruction – this comes on several levels, the physical body, mind, human essence, inner spirit and

Mother Earth. When the Earth had rested and humans slowly returned to their daily lives, for most of them it was a new normal, letting go of some of the old ways. Many had appreciation again of what they called the little things in life. Wounds were healed; families reunited, and love flowed like never before around their planet.

When the virus cycles were over, and the humans were all released from the restraints of the situation, there was a huge energy surge of positive vibration from Earth. Humans recognised the simple gesture of a body-to-body hug was missed. This is because they missed the exchanging of the healing body energy that came with it. When two humans who love and care for each other hug, they do it with the intent of love from the heart. This is a very powerful, pure energy and its exchange helps to aid mental and physical body healing. The ascension beings were waiting for and then captured this new energy with their unconditional love vibration.

They harnessed and multiplied this new energy to create a new love vibration frequency for the new Earth. This energy penetrated into all living cells and a new age began. Freylen also observed that while the world was changing the old Earth frequencies, the 3D heavy, darker side of life energy, was still existing but shrinking. Crimes were less as the years passed, as human lives became more balanced and fairer. She also added to our notes that as Earth approached 2050, criminals were rehabilitated by mind meditation and mindfulness, as well as counselling. The world addiction abuse that existed in the first awakening year of 2020 was nearly non-existent and humanity had worked hard to eradicate this. Serious physical and mind illnesses became less and less as humanity developed clean energy and ways of life. Law and order were still needed as this

Earth was still living in the heavy 3D energy plane, but they had now shifted their world into the 4D energy wave of the new Earth frequency.

I love Freylen's insights and the way we work together, but we were quite tired from all the information we were absorbing and felt it was time for a break from studies and to pamper ourselves.

Life Journal – transmission 21
New Earth - The light beyond the horizon

We took the next light day off and headed for Myclinksan health centre. It was situated on the planet's surface, at the foot of the hills by the outer biosphere that's still in place to protect our city if needed. The biospheres were built during the time of the old weather system called Zelicann. The decision was made to keep them in place just in case of another unforeseen atmosphere emergency.

The health centre overlooks heated springs, and the multi coloured liquids that swell up from the grounds have healing and soothing capabilities. We bathed in the springs and afterwards had relaxing massages from head to foot, before treating ourselves to a delicious lunch. The health centre is set in wonderful grounds, which we took advantage of by choosing to walk the beautiful art trail through the landscaped gardens and lakes. Alas it was just a short respite, but this was enough to refresh us for the next light day of Earth studies.

We reconvened, now looking forward to Earth's time of 2050 to 2100, which saw fifty years of major changes. The awakening had triggered a lot of new thought processes, for example the way humans lived and the imbalance of poverty on the planet. In the 2020-2040 time period, poverty areas on Earth still relied on organisations called charities to survive, and this involved some humans donating their money and time while others chose to ignore it. There were still the odd misplaced populations fleeing old war-torn cities and famine due to the climate change crisis. By the time of 2070, most of the poverty areas had developed into healthy, viable communities that could basically sustain themselves with fewer imports from around the world.

With the on-going effects of climate change, it had become apparent by 2050 that the Earth could not feed the forever growing population. This led to the countries of the world making a joint global decision to keep their individual populations from growing too quickly. It was agreed that births had to be controlled to no more than two per couple. Now this subject was discussed for many years, as some humans saw the new controls as taking away their rights. But the Earth was still in an irreversible extinction crisis and most of humanity eventually realised something had to be done to ensure its future survival.

This led to scientists using their knowledge to look at sustainable ways of growing food, which in turn led to each community and dwelling being responsible for their own crops. Small homes could grow plants inside or outside on living wall plant structures, either in natural or artificial light, and small space was no longer an issue. In addition, all new dwellings were given inside and outside space for this purpose. Communities decided who would grow a particular vegetable or fruit, creating a variety of produce that could be swapped or traded.

By 2055, many of the world's people no longer ate meat, and humans had become mostly vegetarian or vegan. There was no mass animal livestock farming any more, and communities kept their own animals for their needs such as milk and eggs. The cruelty to animals from the Earth's old slaughter methods were now seen as barbaric and disgusting and many could not believe their parents had allowed this by continuing to eat meat. The farm grazing lands instead became organic plant farms, growing crops such as corn, potatoes, rape seed or sugar cane - these were grown for their polylactic acids, which aided the making of clothes and bio gradable storage materials as well as food. Fruit, nuts and vegetables were still traded around the world so all humans could enjoy a variety of nourishment. Leading up to this, a long conservation process had been in place to protect the world bees and pollinating insects from chemicals. This had also contributed to governments encouraging organic farms. Science had now progressed so that perishable goods could be stored for longer life without the use of chemicals.

Freylen has just prompted me to add here that all children on Earth being born in the years after the awakening were there to witness this change on earth. Part of their purpose was to build on the work their parents had put in place for humanity's survival to create this new organic life.

Within this time period, humans looked at how they could build their cities, towns, dwellings and communities. The new buildings no longer dominated the skylines. Lower structures were created that blended with the landscapes around them and were self-sustainable. They had developed new biodegradable building materials that could reflect heat, hold in heat and not pollute the lands when they were no longer needed – everything was designed to be recyclable. All new dwellings had land and self-harnessing energy technology to support a sustainable lifestyle, keep warm and grow food. Across the cities in the world, old office space was adapted to new living accommodation with sustainable low energy at the forefront of all plans. Recycling was part of their daily existence, even including human waste; they had created self-composting facilities for all dwellings that condensed the waste and was used for fertilising the soil or taken away for manufacturing purposes. Leisure and family time were now top of the agenda for healthy minds and bodies. More people were encouraged to create ways of life that kept them at home, exchanging goods for goods and skills for skills. There was still worldwide trade but on a smaller scale, and humans still loved to travel their planet to visit its beauty spots. In all honesty, the records show the human race became more home orientated and discovered they lived very happily in smaller communities.

By 2060 the old travel systems were no longer in existence and the overseers had allowed humanity to expand its technology for gravitational clean energy. This new technology quickly became the most popular way for humans to travel locally and around the world. Various vehicles such as air, sea and land vessels were designed that used clean energy and could travel at high speed if needed. In some ways the world became smaller as a twelve-hour flight would now only take two. The overseers realised this would also lead to space travel for humanity, as human minds now had greater clarity and understanding of the universe. By 2070 humans also had an understanding of possible ways of travelling through light frequency portals, but they had not yet had all the downloaded knowledge components to complete this. The overseers felt that they needed to let humanity evolve in the new Earth frequency at a steady pace so they were not overwhelmed and could make true clear decisions for the human race. A global council had developed, and its members came from all the cultures on Earth. The Global Unity Council – GUC – led the way by this time, making sure humanity did not revert to its old ways.

I see from the Earth records that an exciting time for humans came when the first manned spaceship went to Mars and was followed by further visits. They discovered evidence from their explorations of ascension life that had once been present there, including undercity remains and fragments of cultures on the surface. This really fired their imagination and pushed the desire of scientists to build spaceships that could take them out of their solar system. The old Earth space program had been shut down when the awakening happened due to the collapse of Earth's financial systems, but it was revealed the program already had UFO technology. Since the 1950s of Earth's timeline, humans had been developing limited space travel, but the moon was the physical human limit that was allowed due to humanity's destructive nature. One of the reasons for this was some ascension beings and their mother ships were positioned out near the planets of Saturn and Jupiter, who needed to remain shielded from humanity until they were ready to accept these beings into their lives without fear.

As we approach the years of 2080 to 2100, we see this was an important time for Artificial intelligence (AI). AI had been around for years and humans had always tried to build it in the form of humanity. There was an underlying fear amongst humanity of AI replacing humans, but this was not the way the overseers wanted scientists to progress with this knowledge. The AI robots had come on a long way, but the overseers led humanity to developing body parts with intelligence, designed to interact with the human mind. For example, a new AI leg with skin tissue grown from the patient's living cells could be fitted to the human. The robotic limb and living tissue would connect with the nerve endings and muscles that receive messages from and to the brain. The human could even feel pain if the limb were injured; this technology was also extended to Earth's animal population. For the biological, physical human body, they had the knowledge to re-grow tissue and organs from human cells. Transplants from healthy humans or dying humans were a thing of the past. This did lead to humans living longer, most averaging from 90 to on average 125 years of age. Many mental and physical diseases on earth had disappeared as the world awakened. The new mindset of humans eradicated the negative energy that attacked human cells causing a lot of these illnesses. On top of that the cleansing of the food chain really helped as the chemicals no longer were used that affected human's health.

Freylen observed that humans had learnt not to attach their minds to the image they had of their world, and see it instead as it really was. They had developed new clarity, understanding that thinking of self brought pain and anger, whilst thinking of others brought joy and greater unity. The awakening had brought forward ancient Earth teachings that had always been there, set down in the Buddhist and Tibetan understanding of spiritual life. She observed that in the past, a country called India had many religions within their societies but had mainly lived in spiritual peace with each other. Yet other societies such as Israel, for example, had warred with the Palestinians over land occupation and their religious rights of ownership. The Jewish people wanted to return to a land of Zion, to create a haven away from centuries of persecution. The awakening created a worldwide balance of spiritual understanding for all communities by this time period.

I quickly reflect here that it is wonderful to see the awakening continued to grow and humans were finally living the clean and healthy life they deserved. They had shifted into the fourth dimensional way of thinking and living. They were now stepping into the fifth dimensional clarity of understanding.

Life Journal – transmission 22
New Earth - The light beyond the horizon

As I welcomed this beautiful light day, I heard from Baltrexn; his ship is returning in few light days for a break, so the crew can see families and friends. We were both very excited. I asked him if he wanted to go anywhere specific, but he just wants to stay near to our home dwelling and catch up with everyone. Siroian was going to join him, which pleased Freylen, and it was agreed he would stay at her dwelling so we could all have some private time. This could not have come at a better time, just before I start my incarnation journey. Mind you, I do carry on with my normal life while in the incarnation process but will spend a lot of time observing my Earth life, and this will distract from my time with Baltrexn if he is here during this time period.

I also had a meeting this light day with my incarnation team. When we arrived, everyone was there and we could sense a lot of high vibration in our energies as it would not be long now before the process began. I was advised I would have to come in for pre-evaluation mental and physical tests to make sure I was in good health for this Earth adventure. When the incarnation link was established, I would spend a few days at the centre, then when everyone was happy with the balance of reflection of self and the human form, I could return to my home life. I would then carry on mainly from home, observing my reflection of self and what my Earth life host was experiencing. I would go to the centre for updates and Earth life evaluations as needed. The best way I can describe this experience is to liken it to tuning into a video link, with access to mind-to-mind contact with my guide supporters like Freylen. I will not physically go off-world during this experience as it is important we keep a stable link at all times within the portal, and distance space travel could affect this.

As I had a couple of light days until Baltrexn arrived home, I decided to finish my studies of the last hundred years 2100-2200. My incarnation year is 2222, so this is vital knowledge for the experience I am prepping for.

The universal knowledge revealed that as Earth emerged into the twenty second century of 2100, humans no longer talked of 'the awakening' as an event of daily life as this was now their past history. They were eighty years on now and living the positive consequences of this global event. This was part of every child's teaching, alongside meditation and new universal teachings. The new century brought a new revived positive energy surge, just as new centuries always brought new hope to the pattern of humanity's way of thinking. Even though the world was now tinkering with the fifth dimensional existence of clarity that would open the universal knowledge portals, there was still that doubt with the human mind. Some humans were still holding onto the old energy 3D matrix appearance of things, as well as situations like doubt and fear. A small minority had not ascended yet into the truthful reality of the new Earth energy. If you know our planet's history from Touliza's time, you'll know it is the doubt energy that stops full ascension. When we overcame this and just allowed and trusted the flow of the positive vibration, we eliminated the negative fear energy of doubt, then we ascended and became physical multidimensional beings.

In the year 2133 there was an amazing event on Earth that in some ways shook humanity to the core – they had their first physical encounter for nearly two centuries with ascension beings. Since the awakening, many ascension beings from the Intergalactic Council had continued to telepathically communicate with humans, encouraging them and guiding them in the trance state and visions. They also continued to channel their words through the Earth's written teachings. The overseers and Intergalactic Council now felt it was time for humanity to think about being part of the Intergalactic Council in the future. The starting point to any planet for this is an introduction to one or more of the Intergalactic Council's race of beings. The purpose of this is to build a friendship of trust and exchange of knowledge that would help humanity work within the five-dimensional Earth energies. I saw this was considered as a time of testing the waters, making sure humanity was ready.

This is the role of Baltrexn's ship; it carries ambassadors who make that first contact with the chosen planet or realm, slowly building a relationship of trust.

I felt quite excited as I read about this momentous occasion, which was led by the Pleiadian race. They first chose to appear on the Earth in an area called Tibet, an ancient society of spiritual energy connection and growth. They communicated with the Global Unity Council leaders and set the designated landing site as a meeting place. The world was in awe of these beautiful beings and met them mostly with acceptance that they only came in peace. There was some disruption in odd communities around the world with that fear-based energy of doubt, the fear of the unknown. But the overseers now felt that with Earth's advanced space technology, and the way humanity now lived mostly in a spiritual existence of kindness, love and understanding of each other, they could cope with meeting the Pleiadians. These beings had guided them for thousands of years. Part of this contact was to reveal to humanity their centuries-long involvement with Earth. They brought forward visual evidence of transmissions to humanity to help their understanding.

Freylen said she has studied this in her world teachings, where it is taught as an example of how worlds can change, and how you must never give up hope on anything or anyone. The Pleiadians have been the championing ambassadors of Earth for centuries, always having faith that one day the human race would see the light. The Pleiadian race adapted well to the Earth atmosphere as they had Freylen's ability to adapt to different atmospheric conditions. They returned to their renewal energy life pods as needed, to regenerate their energy on board their spaceship. It helped them that Earth's atmospheric pollution conditions were a thing of the past and purer air and nourishment was available.

We researched the reason the decision was made for this physical contact; the records show that humans had now produced spacecraft with the ability for long, sustainable flights. The Intergalactic Council did not want them randomly leaving their solar system without them having an understanding of the universe from a higher perspective. They could guide Earth on their purpose for exploring their solar system and beyond. Humans needed a directive, say for science or meeting fellow beings, with whom they could exchange goods or knowledge. They had also reached a stage in their clarity and understanding of living in unity, helping and supporting each other and no longer harming Mother Earth. When a species is invited to be part of the Intergalactic Council, a certain criteria must be fulfilled. When the decision is made to invite the chosen species, there is a slow introduction, so they are not overwhelmed by all the species of beings in the universe. A small Earth council was set up to introduce the Intergalactic Council and their protocols, the Global Unity Galactic Council (GUGC). This facilitated liaison between the two parties, who both reported back to the main Intergalactic Council on the progress being made.

The Intergalactic Council knew there would be many questions to answer, and at the top of this list were the explanations for why Earth in the past had been used for so many experiments. I see that understanding was reached with this question, especially when in the last one hundred years or so, so much had been done to support humanity. I also see that the humans felt a bit lost, asking if they now had control of their own destiny. Well I see the answer was yes, if they could abide by the intergalactic protocols.

This is a simple breakdown for you in the Earth language of these protocols:

- Respect of the Intergalactic Council, overseers and all species who are part of the light in the universe.

- First contact can only be made when the prime directive is given by the Intergalactic Council. This means they have studied the sentient species and culture and considered them for approach at a suitable point of their evolution. Some sentient species will be left to live in accordance with its normal cultural evolution if deemed not ready.

- Have an understanding of the overseers' high ascension knowledge and decisions made for the benefit of the universe. Being allowed to respectfully question these decisions so all parties can reach a unity of understanding and learning.

- Respecting those you engage with and each other's beliefs, cultures and uniqueness, and all living by true spiritual values:

  - Kindness
  - Honesty
  - Love
  - Compassion
  - Gratitude
  - Supporting others
  - Friendship
  - Non judgement
  - Selflessness
  - Empathy

- Science and technology knowledge may only be exchanged with other cultures if the Intergalactic Council and the recipient agree it will be beneficial to their way of life. All actions are to be for the greater good of all.

- Awareness of combat with dark forces is vital – engaging with the dark forces will not take place without the agreement of the Intergalactic Council. If your lives are in instant danger and there is no other choice, then the Intergalactic Council will respect the choice and review the events that created the situation. Full enquiry will result in this latter action.

- To share your cultural teachings and knowledge with the universal library so that other cultures may seek knowledge from it when they are ready.

By 2150 the relationship with the Pleiadians had been profoundly established and the new history of Earth would never be the same again.

Life Journal – transmission 23
New Earth - The light beyond the horizon

I welcomed yet another break from my studies as Baltrexn arrived home. Siroian came with him as Freylen was here studying with me when they arrived at the portal travel station. We all caught up with each other again over a lovely meal. Baltrexn told us about a new species they had made contact with. They were called Codumians and they were what you would understand as a changeling physical structure species. They were of a human physical make up, but they could link into their multidimensional cell structure and morph. This allowed them, while in the physical state, to be able to blend completely with their surroundings and not be seen.

They had been a species that many off-world dark forces had tried to conquer, to force them to use their morphing ability for war purposes and spying. A physical weapon that could morph would make the ideal spy, creating a position of powerful advantage in any tactical warfare of domination. Sadly, over their time many Codumians had been captured, some never to be seen again. Despite this, some had managed to return eventually, revealing information about other worlds and species. Their morphing ability had also saved many from being taken by force. The younglings were the main targets for capture as this physical morphing was a change that took place in them at the age of puberty. It is like a puberty of development in their physical form, when chemical change is triggered, which allows them to evolve this unique gift. This was the age when they understood the world around them and what their morphing abilities would mean to themselves and their people.

Baltrexn's ship was passing through their solar system when the Codumians saw it was an intergalactic ship and reached out for help, seeking their protection. Baltrexn explained they were now under the Intergalactic Council's protection and would gain from its vast knowledge. He describes a beautiful, unique planet of wonder, and it fascinated him when he could walk into a space and the Codumians would emerge from their backgrounds! Over their expanse of time they had developed a telepathic link with this ability. This was used if they were in danger; when they morphed, they could silently tell each other when it was safe to emerge. Baltrexn explained they lived in simple village settings, at one with their planet. They had advanced communication technology, and objects like sky scopes to see their stars and galaxy. They had not yet built craft to leave their planet as they were afraid of being targeted off-world. Through their contact with other species who sought to steal their ability, they had learned much about the universe. This is how they knew of the Intergalactic Council, that they fought the dark forces, and would protect them. It was quite a heartrending story and we were so pleased this unique race had been able to seek and find the protection it needed.

We spent the following light day with our parents, enjoying the family bonding time. Siroian and Freylen also joined us. We met up at my parents' home, a large dwelling set in a beautiful garden. As well as the usual sleeping and resting rooms, they have a meditation chamber and a large creation room for my mother's garment making. We had a splendid lunch with several courses of delicious foods. My mother had made the effort to try and create a Pleiadian dish which delighted Siroian and Freylen.

These two light days with my beloved Baltrexn went too quickly, but we used it wisely to plan our future. We had been bonded for ten hyons, with our lives fully focused on ourselves and our bonded relationship. We made the decision that after my incarnation experience, we would have a youngling. We knew the upbringing would be more down to me to focus on as Baltrexn travelled so much, and I would have to limit my work for a while. But something inside me was ready for this life-giving event and to give to another all I have in body, mind and spirit. The other exciting news was that Freylen and Siroian were what modern Earth language would call an item. I cannot tell you how pleased we are, we knew they were destined for each other and I can see the love reflecting out from their eyes and their beating hearts.

Life Journal – transmission 24
New Earth - The light beyond the horizon

After two days of fun with Baltrexn, it was time to refocus on my Earth mission, while he returned to his light ship to start a new mission of his own. This light day I had a meeting with my incarnation team as it is not long now until my incarnation mission starts and we are all getting excited at the prospect. Afterwards, I had to stay for my pre-incarnation tests. I was checked for my physical health and mental endurance. They also tested me at a cellular level for the multidimensional body split. This is something all Diacuratians can do, which means while still in a physical body my ethereal conscious self can travel to other destinations off-world. This is restricted by the Intergalactic Council, only to places under their care, and each traveller has to state the reason for going. I can only travel if I have this approval, or else I will be prevented and returned to my planet. It was explained to me that this process helps keep order and balance in a vast universe, as well as keeping you safe. It also allows me to travel through portals and the physical self reappears at the other end intact. Baltrexn's star ship can go into multidimensional transition frequency for long distant space travel, and the bodies can adapt to this, still having mind conscious communication to each other.

I am pleased to say I passed all the tests with flying colours and Havrium is going to set the date for the incarnation process to begin. Meanwhile I have to finish off my Earth history research with Freylen.

After the first physical contact in 2133, the relationship between humans and Pleiadians grew from strength to strength. By 2150 there was an Earth alliance established with the Intergalactic Council. It took a few years to build a solid trust foundation mainly because some humans had trouble accepting these beautiful alien beings. As I said earlier it caused quite a reaction, with a few billion people having to reset many centuries of old belief systems. Through perseverance from both sides, this was achieved by explaining the history of Earth with ascension beings, as I have revealed in these transmissions. It gave the green light for Earth to become part of the Intergalactic Council. The Pleiadians gave evidence of these facts, revealing the universal knowledge library to the global leaders of Earth. The global leaders could then feed this to the public to help their understanding of their universe. As you can imagine this was a big ask for humans to absorb. I could relate to this as our history shows a similar thing happened to Diacuratians when the overseers came with a Calentian crystal of knowledge many hyons ago.

Over the next fifty years, humanity slowly started to spread out into their own solar system and galaxy. This created the foundation for further travel one day into the deep space of the universe. They started by creating a base on Mars and learning about their own solar system. Human scientists had to adjust to new learning as new knowledge allowed them to understand the universe more. Their limited third dimensional way of thinking had been altered to bring greater clarity.

They were slowly introduced to a few other species of the Intergalactic Council who had been part of Earth's history. Humans had made the fourth-dimension breakthrough and were starting to live in a fifth dimensional understanding. They were not capable yet of multidimensional split, but they were bordering on telepathic communication between human to human. Working with the Pleiadians had enhanced this, especially with the humans who meditated, creating mind clarity and working at this connection daily.

Humans still lived in self-sustaining communities with schools and natural medicine healing centres. They also now had dedicated schools that focused on meditation and telepathic education. With the advance space travel programme in place, space academies were created for adults to train for a life in space. Many roles were required for a spaceship to function, from medical teams to engineers. The larger spaceship could accommodate families with a school for education while aboard. The humans that chose not to enter this new space life stayed on Earth, living a very spiritual, holistic existence.

One of the big changes was that religions self-evaluated and altered, merging into a one world belief system, not called a religion anymore. This transformation had been created from a greater spiritual understanding of existence brought to them by this new off-world knowledge. This built on the years of the awakening period from 2020, opening the gates to enlightenment. I see my incarnation was going to be in the time period of exciting continued growth for this amazing new Earth. I also realised that as they ascended into the fifth dimension the incarnation programme might not be needed on Earth anymore.

Life Journal – transmission 25
New Earth - The light beyond the horizon

The light day has finally arrived for the process of my incarnation mission to start. I have just arrived at the mind and body travel centre where the reflection of self-body splits for incarnation is to take place. I have packed for a few light days; as I said earlier, I have to stay to make sure all is stable with the incarnated Earth soul before I can return home.

I was greeted by Havrium who took me to my resting room adjacent to the multidimensional room, to unpack and settle in. I then had a tour of the multidimensional room where the refection of self-split will take place. I was reminded as I looked around how much technology has moved on since the pioneering days of Touliza. In her day the incarnation split took place in an observation pod bed, with a clear energy cover that moved over her and gently rotated to monitor her physical form and mind vital signs. I was now observing an upright tube where I will be held in a suspended energy field while the split takes place. There were various workstations and a small observation platform in the room. Uculium, the multidimensional split specialist, and Ourriyn, who monitors the higher self, which is me, were there already preparing for the next light day. The next light day was a day of testing and making sure all technology was set to my body frequency and the Earth child I was incarnating into.

I want you to understand how the power of my mind is involved in this process. This is the power of the intent of thought, which helps me choose destinations for multidimensional travelling. Also understand the power of the full multidimensional energy link connecting the mind to the physical body, which enables you to maintain the link throughout separation. The intent is set at the highest energy matrix of the twelfth dimension, and links back through all dimensions, stopping at the reference point of existence you are in. Imagine silver threads from the divine source, which your multidimensional body is tethered to, weaving their way through the cosmic universe to your physical body. This powerful thought cannot be broken unless the mind setting the event chooses it, the physical body dies during multidimensional travelling, or another being of high ascension energy links to your frequency to intervene if you are in danger. This is how I hold the link with my reflection of self, known on Earth as the soul. When the split occurs my state of mind and intentions must be pure, fully wanting this to happen.

The combination of my mind and technology works together to create the soul for the journey to Earth. The technology uses a mixture of light and harmonic sound energy, alongside my power of thought to create my reflection of self. Havrium had already explained the three selves present in the Earth humanoid form. The actual self is the physical body's everyday functioning mind – pretty much everything they think and do. The body self is the physical realisation of the 'I am', although it works in conjunction with the actual self. The higher self is the observer and evaluator of the other two selves, me, the incarnated energy linking with me. When all three are working in balance, a species copes and moves in harmony of life. To create this harmony, it is vital the incarnation transition is balanced.

We did some more tests on my body frequencies and then I was advised to rest before the next light day when the split will take place. I managed to mind link with Baltrexn, who was very excited for me. He was looking forward to hearing about my Earth life and adventures.

Life Journal – transmission 26
New Earth - The light beyond the horizon

The next light day, we gathered in the multidimensional room with the mission team and some observers from our sacred light council. I could feel an underlying excitement, as well as the seriousness of this incarnation mission to Earth. I had already had it explained to me what would happen next, which would involve me linking with a humanoid form conceived on Earth; they also explained that not all human babies survive birth, or can pass away just after, in very rare cases.

I have already mentioned the reflection of self, so I thought I would explain this further to you. It is not an identical copy of my multidimensional ethereal body, but more of a reflection of myself, that is linked to me at all times. My reflection of self will be a multidimensional vessel that will be the gatherer of knowledge and information from my incarnated life on the Earth plane. We will be linked at all times, but I will choose when to connect and see the progression of my physical Earth life. My guides and observers, like Havrium, will also be reviewing my progress. Everything for your understanding is recorded, including the mind links to the Earth body. When my reflection of self returns at the end of my Earth life, everything is reviewed and downloaded into our transmission library and uploaded to the intergalactic universal knowledge library. I will then reconnect with my reflection of self.

I plan to continue transmitting my Earth life to my journal transmissions in the current format, choosing the key moments to share with you whilst living my Diacuratian existence. The full life transmission will be available separately on the universal knowledge library, relaying every moment and feeling of that Earth lifetime for those who wish to study it.

As I stood waiting for the process to begin, I watched all the serious faces and their frowns of concentration. This was a momentous occasion for me, even though I had gathered knowledge on what I could expect to experience, I know you only truly experience something when you go through it yourself.

Eventually I was asked to step into the monitoring pod that would observe my physical body functions. I felt my physical form being lifted and then I was suspended in mid-air, floating in a light harmonic energy field. I felt calm and my physical form slowed down, and I was asked to separate into my multidimensional self. I then had to transport my multidimensional self in the light harmonic sound particle transmitter. This is an open, round column space, and when I entered it, I was surrounded by a light harmonic sound beam. My multidimensional self was being monitored at the same time as my physical self. They observe the energy link between physical and ethereal form by monitoring my energy frequency vibration, which is unique for every being in the universe, and make sure it stays stable.

While the light harmonic beam surrounded me, I could feel my ethereal self pulsating. My mind was focused on the thought intent of the split, which would create a reflection of me. Then I heard a sound that was new to me and the light beams started to throb and spin around me. I felt as if someone was pulling at my energy and I heard a voice in my mind telling me to release; I was meant to have no expectations, trust and go with the feelings that came across me. I felt myself change, felt a bit weaker than normal, that it was taking everything I had to stay focused. Then I felt the light harmonic sound beams slow and clear, I was still suspended in the energy, and I was left to rest for a bit.

The room was a hive of activity. In the middle of the room, there was a light being that was an energy reflection of me. The form was different to my multidimensional self; it was like a floating, pulsating ball of light. I could feel it was part of me and was connected to my mind, I could see what my self-reflection was feeling and seeing. Havrium said I would telepathically connect to my reflection of self as I do to any physical being, but as well as hearing communication in my mind I would see images of where they were. I can also control when this happens as I lead my normal life on Diacurat.

The next stage was to place my energy connection reflection of self into the chosen humanoid foetus on Earth and test that everything was functioning as it should be. It had already been explained to me that for the humanoid form, the best way of blending with the foetus was gradually, over a few Earth weeks. By week twenty-four of a human pregnancy, the foetus is usually fully formed, and at this point, the reflection of self will be blended to a point of balance within the human baby that is safe. During the weeks that the incarnated energy is gaining strength, I will be connecting, observing what my refection self can feel and see. I cannot express to you in words how much I am looking forward to this unique experience.

Life Journal – transmission 27
New Earth - The light beyond the horizon

Following the split of my multidimensional self it was normal to monitor the three energies for a while – my physical body, multidimensional self and reflection of self, to make sure all was stable. This would take a couple of our light days.

The exciting moment had arrived, and it was now time for me to blend my reflection of self with the Earth baby. In Touliza's time they used a light way portal to reach Earth in a light star ship, and from there, her reflection of self blended with the baby. The light star ship was at the fifth physical dimensional level, created for helping fifth dimensional species in these procedures. It had similar chambers to those set up in her time on Diacurat in the Temple. But technology had moved on and through mind control with my selected guides and myself, they could now transport the soul through the transitional dimensional layers of the universe to the Earth child. The reflection of self is held in an energy field and it had been explained to me that they would not place all of my reflection of self into the baby at one go, as the blending with the physical form within the womb could have a bad reaction. As the baby grows, more of my refection of self will be slowly filtered into the human form. The master scientists have found that the soul within split between human and spirit becomes balanced within the human form, although the time this event takes place can be different for each human. It can be in childhood or adulthood depending on their life's mission.

The best way I can describe this is that they transmit the soul in ethereal multidimensional energy portions as needed. The reflection of self travels through the light harmonic sound technology transporter to my Earth body, all binding together in an energy force that protects and transmits the reflection of self to its destination. The mission technicians keep a continued watch over this process, guiding the soul's energy. This does not affect me as my reflection of self has been captured in an energy force field. We will be tuning into my reflection of self which is held in the force field.

The chamber was silent as this was carried out; only those that were to help with connecting to the physical form were present, and my first journey in an incarnated Earth form began. My reflection of self was in the light harmonic sound technology transporter. I felt my own energy alter but remained connected to my reflection of self and my guiding group. My thoughts were as one with them, and we shared the experience with my reflection of self as it went to the chosen Earth being in his mother's womb. I then felt my connection shift, going to an image of a young life growing in a human womb, then I saw a light, which was the soul connecting. I felt a whoosh of energy shoot through me, then all was calm, and I could hear the heartbeat of my physical Earth form.

Throughout my mission with this physical form, I will be supported by Havrium, Uculium, Ourriyn and Ionkul, who will be giving me and my soul energy in the Earth child guidance and healing. This is to ensure my own physical body stays in balance with my mind and maintains the stable link to my reflection of self. My close guides will be Freylen, Oucustion and Pactsaceon, and they will be guiding my life mission.

I was aware of everything the baby was feeling, from his cellular structure, physical sensations, his blood pumping through his veins, and his developing mind feelings, which extended to awareness of the world outside the womb. All of this information was being fed back to me, as my reflection of self is like a recording sponge, soaking up all that happens. When my reflection of self was stable, we all drew back our energy and the team could then monitor over the next few earth weeks the completion of the connection using the light harmonic sound technology transporter. My reflections of self's transmissions of energy were now going to be collected by the mission group, who could also watch my Earth life as it progressed. But what was of real interest to the master scientists was to see how I would feel and respond to my incarnated reflection of self – known by the humans on Earth as a soul.

My reflection of self was incarnated into a foetus, known on Earth as a baby, who was named Alaric by his Earth parents – which on their planet means all-powerful king or ruler. The Earth year of my birth was 2222. He was the first child of a couple who lived in an area called Provence in a country called France. They were a hard-working family on the lands growing organic food. His father was Jonas and his mother was known as Yulia. More will be revealed soon about my Earth family in my transmissions.

My first observation was how tranquil the being Alaric felt – he had no past or future thoughts or expectations; he was living in the now moment of reality in the womb. He could only feel the unconditional love of source from me and his mother. I observed he also felt vibrations from the outside world coming through the womb, but as yet, they had no meaning for him. I realised baby humanoids have no preconceived ideas; he would enter the Earth world dependent on his parents for survival. I can relate this to our own world, and it is similar for many physical existing species across the universe.

I now had to wait patiently for when the newborn baby chose to leave the womb and start his new life on his Earth path. I felt fine, even though a part of my energy was leaving for a period of time to be in the physical Earth form, and I felt comforted by knowing we would always be connected.

I was aware that when the child is born, his soul – my reflection of self – could leave the physical body while he slept and explore the Earth and its fourth dimensional planes. In other words, the soul is not cocooned for the Earth years in the moments we spend within the physical body. The term given to this is astral travelling, and all the incarnated souls can have outer body experiences while the human form is sleeping or in a deep meditative state. As I said, I can spend time in the fourth dimension astral plane and connect with my fifth dimension energy friends. My reflection of self is tethered to his Earth body as my ethereal energy is to mine.

When the mission team were happy with everything, I left to go to my resting space. I was going to contact Baltrexn, but I must have been very tired as I fell straight away into a dreamless sleep.

Life Journal – transmission 28
New Earth - The light beyond the horizon

As I enter this light day my senses have now fully recovered from yesterday, and I have clarity regarding my experience. The incarnation process affected my physical body more than I realised it would and I slept all night, which is apparently very common. I immediately contacted Baltrexn to let him know I was ok, but Havrium had contacted him to let him know it all went well and I was grateful for this kind thought.

After I refreshed my body and had some nourishment, I entered the multidimensional room, which was very quiet. I could see my reflection of self in its chamber, where it will stay suspended until all is filtered to complete Alaric's soul's energy connection.

Later on, Freylen, Oucustion and Pactsaceon arrived to meet about their guide roles and my life mission. For many centuries, the soul and higher self had planned their life's journeys while incarnating, to gain knowledge for their own ascension. Also, their purpose was to help Earth's energies, to help them ascend out of the third dimensional existence and help Mother Earth. Now that humanity was ascending into the fifth dimensional energies, the latter was more of a priority of the Intergalactic Council. Humanity had reset its way of thinking to live in a world unity of support and kindness. The incarnated soul's purpose was to enhance this energy and bring humanity to its full potential. This would work alongside the spiritual foundation the Pleiadians had built with humanity and continued to build every Earth day. So, my overall Earth life's mission was to be part of the Pleiadians' support for the planet. We had set this into Alaric's life path, which will be revealed in my future transmissions. In the course of his life, more guides will join our team as they are needed.

Also, for future transmission understanding, I remind you that the lengths of our light days vary between the two planets, and we are in a different reality and dimension. Every one of our light days is seven Earth months in the understanding of time dimensional light frequency differences. I will be tuning in every light day to see how his life is progressing and support my reflection of self. I can try to influence his decisions to keep the life mission on track, as will my support guides.

Now, as I am a female of my species, you might think it odd for me to incarnate into a male of the human Earth species. I was given the option a while ago and decided I would like to experience the male energy of Earth. I had connected to the transmissions of our pioneer, Touliza, on her incarnation to a female called Aigle. Part of these transmissions allow you to experience some of the sensation frequencies that were passed to her from her reflection of self. I wanted to be different, and see and experience a different energy, and the lessons this will bring.

Life Journal – transmission 29
New Earth - The light beyond the horizon

I have been monitoring Alaric's life so far in the womb; there is not much to report apart from his steady body growth and his perception of noise from the world outside. But I am excited as we have reached a momentous light day, as Alaric will be born from his mother's womb on Earth. For this occasion, we gathered at the multidimensional centre, to witness him take his first breath. The soul is monitored closely at this event in Earth time and when he is born more of my reflection of self is blended with him.

The labour, as earthlings call this event, started with Yulia's waters breaking. This is a fluid substance that keeps the humanoid sustained with a cord of life from the mother's womb. She then has something called contractions which push the child through the mother's birth canal. I witnessed a few Earth hours of the mother in great pain, but this was greatly eased by the sound and energy healing and herbs she was given while they all waited for this transition of life.

My reflective self, the human soul, was aware of change so I could experience this as the baby's physical body was being squeezed down the birth canal. This was my first sensation of human pain which I experienced as his head emerged into the world. Then his physical body was out, and I felt him take his first breath and express himself vocally to the world around him. With this first breath, I witnessed the transition of life in the womb to breathing the air around him. It was as if the physical body took a pause, accepted transition, and then carried on in this new environment, and it was quite amazing to see. His father Jonas was present for the birth of his son, encouraging his wife through the pain. When Alaric was washed and dressed, he lifted him up and took him outside to see his first sunset. Alaric really was not understanding this as he had already fallen asleep, tired from the birthing, but I felt this was a lovely gesture by a deeply spiritual man.

Alaric had a full head of black hair and blue eyes; he was quite a long baby, which reflected the DNA of his father, who was very tall. His mother was left to rest, tired after her labour, but in good health. She had been attended by the community birthing doctor and her own mother, grandmother to Alaric.

I had already seen that Alaric's grandmother was a very spiritual woman. The meaning of her name, Aceso, reflected what she was in life, a healer of her community, and she had passed her knowledge on to her daughter Yulia. Alaric's grandfather had already left the Earth plane, his incarnated soul returning home. He had been killed in a tragic accident while riding his horse, and I gather from listening to conversations that he was a kind family man who loved his organic farm. Jonas had taken over the farm on his death, having previously been an engineer on a travel machines. But he had also been brought up on a farm; as they say on Earth, this was in his blood, and his engineering knowledge did come in handy when the farming machinery broke down. These were solar powered vehicles that could harvest the various crops alongside AI robots that worked as farm hands and helped to process the food. The advancement of AI on Earth had been significant; these robots were part of the family and had their own dwelling to live in and recharge themselves when needed. Families still did not have more than one or two children to help with the world's population, which stood at under five billion humans at this point in time. The population had dropped dramatically over two hundred years, through climate change, natural disasters and human birth control.

My observations of Alaric have been very interesting, and I am getting to know his family and their position in their community's society. Their farm is on the outskirts of the community town and they grow flowers, vegetables and fruit, the region's specialities being apples, apricots, cherries, peaches and plums. As well as providing for the locals they transport their goods to other regions of France and to Italy. With new technology, goods travel quickly in the gravity flying crafts, helping to keep them fresh.

Their main dwelling is all on one level and nearly all the rooms open out onto a large courtyard. Alaric's mother and grandmother love flowers, so in the summer months the courtyard is a picture of nature at its best. This space is used for socialising, eating, cooking and general pleasure. The structure was mainly built from sustainable bamboo, a hard-wearing and versatile material which had been used widely for years.

Also attached to the house is a healing and meditation structure in the shape of a pyramid. It was built with white onyx and a crystalline material. These pyramid structures of various sizes were used across the world at this time, and the family used this sacred energy space for their own body, mind and soul balancing as well as for helping others. All of humanity had great understanding now of the higher self and connecting to the universe consciousness. The Pleiadians had brought their pyramid knowledge to Earth, which had been known in ancient Atlantis and up to the ancient Egyptian period. With the worldwide group meditations now in practice, which had the intention to heal Mother Earth, the planet's energy frequencies were rising into the fifth dimension requirements for ascension. Alaric had been in this pyramid nearly every day since he was born, creating a wonderful aura and balanced chakra system around and within him.

As well as the house dwelling, there were buildings for travel crafts and food storage. They also had general livestock for milk for cheese and eggs that helped to service the community's needs as well as their own.

His mother's and grandmother's favourite place was the walled herb garden, which was where they grew what they needed for natural health remedies. Adjacent to this was a special structured greenhouse building where they made and stored these remedies. They also ran a small export enterprise, as well as supplying the local community.

I could see Alaric was going to grow up in a very busy farm and community. I might have painted a rather idyllic rural life, but technology was commonplace in their lives, evidenced by the AI robots and their modes of transport. They also had the crystal technology for both world-wide and off-world communication. This was handy, as Jonas' elder brother Cael was an officer on an Earth spaceship. He travelled often within the solar system, and often transmitted his adventures to Jonas. I had seen that this was a highlight of an evening's entertainment after a long day on the farm.

Life Journal – transmission 30
New Earth - The light beyond the horizon

I am enjoying this experience so far, although it does feel surreal at times, when I am viewing my incarnated life; while I am absorbed into the images and feelings I am experiencing, I am also aware of how fascinating it is. It has been interesting to observe Alaric's response to people's voices, and seeing his first smile. I've also noticed how quickly they learn to cry for food, or for help when they are not happy or comfortable. They, of course, are dependent on the adults of their world for survival, as are the young on my own planet, and the thousands of other physical life forms which exist in this way throughout the universe.

Freylen has been a big support to me in this process so far, as she can advise me on the sensations and vibrations I experience from my reflection of self. We are both grateful to be busy at this time as Baltrexn and Siroian have gone on a long deep space mission, taking them into another dimensional universe. Because of the distance, they will be gone for a while and we cannot connect with them at the moment, so we are glad of the light day distractions. I have also been transmitting some of my history notes, having been asked to collate them for a virtual knowledge book for the history students of Diacurat to learn from.

During this incarnation mission process, I have regular contact with Alaric's guides Freylen, Oucustion and Pactsaceon. They produce regular reports and all parties involved receive these transmissions. If there are any concerns, we collectively discuss solutions to help Alaric.

As I move forward through his first two years of Earth life, his language has started to develop well. I had no knowledge of the Earth languages, but as all souls and higher selves, we link into this language of birth and quickly understand it. I remember his first steps and observing the encouragement his family gave him to learn to walk tall. It was interesting to watch how young humans learn to balance and take those first steps of trust, which opens up a whole new world to them. I am relating well to this young earthling and so many things are similar to my own young development. Alaric also has learnt to sit for short periods of time in the healing pyramid, he is still a bit fidgety, but Freylen tells me this will soon change and is common in young earthlings.

I had noticed he had an early ability to read minds, but he would not have understood this yet; he seems to pre-sense what others are thinking and what their reactions could be. Many humans were developing this ability, and it was enhanced by the healing-meditation pyramids, which had become a daily routine for them. In one of our catch-up meetings, Pactsaceon said that many of this new generation of Earth beings would have this ability. The Pleiadians and other ascension beings will help humanity harness this new ability for the good of all. He thought within three new generations humanity will have this telepathic communication mastered, which will also lead them to multidimensional separation, which in turn is linked to mind control.

At this wonderful age of two, the world to Alaric was one great big exploration and learning space. Alaric spent much of his day with his mother, following her around like a little shadow. Whatever she was doing on the farm she would talk to him and explain her tasks. She knew that he would be absorbing this knowledge even at such a young age. Also, to my delight, he adored animals of all kinds and showed them great kindness. I felt this was experienced at a deeper level than I had expected from a human. As he learnt to communicate better, he would tell his mother and father if they had something wrong with them or what their needs were, and was often right. We agreed he had an extrasensory perception that was very strong and it would be interesting to see how this would be used throughout his life.

As well as observing Alaric's young life, I was able to study the community and surrounding area. The family farm was a short distance away from the small town that sat at the foot of pretty rolling hills leading to mountains as a backdrop. The town was built up around a river that flowed through it, quite an ancient site that had not altered through the last few centuries. The old buildings were built of natural stone with terracotta tiled roofs, set quite close together along pretty narrow streets. As the town expanded over time, all new buildings were a mix of stone and sustainable materials like bamboo, straw, rammed earth techniques and recycled materials from derelict or unused buildings. They had more space around them, with land for growing family crops and small holdings for domestic animals.

In Alaric's third year in the month of July, on a hot summer's day, his sister was born. He was now the older brother to Vanina, a beautiful baby with a shock of auburn hair. His mother had been telling him he was going to have a little sister soon and he had felt her moving in his mother's tummy. But the day reality dawned was a bit different for him as he saw his parents focus on this new life and not him; he stood back and watched, trying to understand this sudden change in his world. There was a new feeling he did not understand, something I knew was jealousy, which can be very common with young Earth siblings. I realised his parents were ready for this and quickly included him in their daily routines with their new daughter, asking him to help as big brother. I loved the moment when his father Jonas took him aside and said they were both there to protect Vanina, and as big brother, his job was to always help and encourage her. He started to spend more time now with his father and grandmother. I was pleased to see that he embraced this and was now, at the age of three, in need of more variety in life to inspire him.

He was a very bright and intuitive child and had a learning mind like a sponge; Jonas often said to Yulia he reminded him of his brother Cael. One of the things that contributed to this thought was that at this young age, Alaric was fascinated by the stars and loved to look through the sky scope at them, and the planets in their solar system. Jonas remembered his brother being like this, while he was happy to stay on Earth and had never been curious about what was out there, beyond his home planet. Cael had seen Alaric in the flesh when he was six months old and they often saw each other on the communication devices. He always made Alaric beam and Jonas could see they were already developing a close life bond.

Alaric was now at the age his education route was being decided. There were a few methods available – home schooling was very popular on this new Earth, where a teaching robot was used for the lesson periods guided by their parents, and was always based on how the child could reach their full potential. Jonas and Yulia already could tell the farm life would not be enough for their son; he was already seeking knowledge beyond his years of the world and universe around him. There was a communal school in the town that children could go to at the age of six. Society felt this was an ideal age for them to leave their home environment for short periods, as they could emotionally cope with it better. Another option was if the child showed a certain talent like maths, science or the arts; there were schools around the world that took these children and enhanced this, so they could maximise their talents and abilities. There were also schools for children who wanted a space career, like the one Cael had attended. Jonas had missed his brother when he left at the age of twelve for space cadet academy in a country called the United States of America. He came home often which helped, but Jonas soon realised they were so different, and it was important Jonas was happy with his chosen career and life, as he would be staying on the farm.

All teaching methods combined their school days with mindfulness and meditation education, with the spiritual ethos humanity now lived by. Most of the education establishments had human and robot teachers, as humanity did not want their world to become completely led by robotics. They believed there should always be a human element to any education, making sure those teachers had mentally and physically experienced the subject they taught.

Alaric's parents decided to home school him to the age of six, when he would join the local community school. This required a teaching robot to integrate into family life so the two children became used to it being around them. They wanted to give Alaric time to develop his strengths independently. This would ensure they were interpreting him correctly and could then decide the next stage of his education at the ages of six and twelve.

Freylen and I were enjoying this incarnation mission and observing this new caring world that put children's development at the forefront of humanity.

Life Journal – transmission 31
New Earth - The light beyond the horizon

I was excited to wake this light day to a message from Baltrexn. It had been sent just before they travelled thorough the multidimensional portal to the universe they were going to explore. It was a very personal message, saying how much he loved me and would miss me. This touched my heart; I wished I could see where he was and what he was experiencing, and I looked forward to when he could relay his experiences to me. I trusted they would be safe, as many star ships had connected with this universe and had returned safely. This is an important mission, as links are being made with new species and overseers of their kind.

When I met with Freylen later she had also had a message from Siroian, I did not ask her what it said, but from the glint in her eye I suspected it was similar to mine.

Staying focused on the mission in hand, I relayed my observations as Alaric reached his fifth birthday. His younger sister was now his little shadow and following him everywhere she was allowed to. Vanina adored her older brother, and it helped that he was very patient with her. She was a beautiful child with deep auburn hair and ivory skin. She had big green eyes and that often reflected the mischief she got up to, and a contagious laugh full of fun. She adored her grandmother who had started teaching her the herbal healing ways even by the age of two. She felt Vanina was a natural and was very excited at the prospect of teaching her all her own skills. Vanina was also a bright child who showed a lot of future potential, which was yet to be decided. She also loved nature and animals and was showing signs of creativity in making things and painting.

When she was in the healing meditation pyramid, she could sit for a long time and would come back with her garbled words of what she had seen, trying to explain it in her language for the adults to understand.

Alaric's birthday celebrations were fun, and enjoyed with some friends of similar age he had invited over. His grandmother had set up a treasure hunt of sweet delights for them and it was wonderful to hear the excitement and laughter as they discovered their finds. Vanina followed them all but she did not find many, so they all kindly shared with her – in fact, to her delight, she ended up with the most, thanks to their generosity. They played a simple game called hide and seek before it was time for a delicious party tea. It was a hot day that made them all thirsty, and this was quenched with homemade iced lemonade. Alaric received many gifts, but his favourite was one his uncle Cael sent him – a toy model of the star ship he served on. He was fascinated by it and his imagination took him on adventures as he ran around the garden pretending to fly it. It was lovely to witness milestones of his life like this, all captured by my reflection of self.

I had come to realise how important family was in this time period on Earth. In the studies of past centuries there had been times in some western societies when families were not together, and many were estranged. The awakening of over two hundred years ago had contributed to this new way of life. Often, generations lived in the same house or very near to each other, offering the support network that families needed. With sickness basically being a thing of the past now, many humans lived well beyond their nineties, enjoying active lives. If their health started to fail through old age, then the families looked after them until their death. After the soul had returned to its higher self's home of existence, a celebration of their life was held. The body's ashes were given back to the land with a tree often planted in memory of them where the ashes were scattered. The religions of the world were merging into a new spiritual belief system since the Pleiadians had become part of their reality and future. They understood the overseers as what they had perceived as god, and how the ascension beings of Earth's history had influenced humanity's belief systems.

Life Journal – transmission 32
New Earth - The light beyond the horizon

My life is carrying on as normal alongside my incarnation mission, and my connection to reflection of self happens when I choose in my light day. Sometimes it's with Alaric's guides Freylen, Oucustion and Pactsaceon so we can discuss his life and what he and myself are learning from this experience. One of the big changes that will happen around Alaric's twelfth birthday is that there will be a couple of new guides joining us. This is a stage when he will make a big life decision for his future and the new guides will be there to help with this process. They are being selected at the moment so when I know more you will be updated.

My daily pattern has been to tune into my reflection of self after my morning meal, taking note of anything that stands out like life milestones, so I can send these transmissions. I observe feelings and vibrational frequencies of my reflection of self, and the message the soul has been trying to convey to Alaric to guide him. Then later in my light day I tune in again to recap and observe any further changes. If Freylen, Oucustion and Pactsaceon see something they think I should be aware of, they contact me to flag this experience. While I am doing this from my home base Uculium, Ourriyn and Pecion, who I mentioned in an earlier transmission, take it in turns to monitor my reflection of self and my energy frequencies from the mission room at the centre.

I have met regularly with my and Baltrexn's parents to catch up with general life happenings. I cannot reveal to them at the moment about my incarnated life experience, as these are always kept private until after the event. This is so it is my experience and I alone, with Alaric's guides, who make decisions and learn from this in the moment. Later, what we have learned is all processed and eventually released to the universal's knowledge library of incarnation experiences section for others to study. I have also typed up my history notes and they are being edited by the head of the History Faculty at Kihackin History Institute. I do not have much of a social life as lot of my friends are elsewhere on the planet or off-world but luckily, we are a species that likes our own company. Of course, I must not forget my animal friend Peagal, who is loving all the attention he is getting at this time.

Life for Alaric was running smoothly; he was now six and ready to go to school in his town. He had already had an induction day where he met his fellow classmates; classes were kept small, with never any more than twelve. This was so they could all interact well, and gain confidence to ask questions and get the learning they needed. It was also better with fewer pupils so the teachers could easily identify their strengths and weaknesses and action these as appropriate.

I felt the excitement in his young body when the time finally came for his first day at school. He caught the school hover craft that collected all the children – they were encouraged to be independent of their parents from day one. This is because often pupils would go away to study at the age of twelve if they had a talent they could specialise in. If a pupil did not wish to study further afield, they went back to their home teaching, studying their chosen trade to serve the community. But saying that, I could see that anyone could change their life's path and restudy at any age if it helped the higher purpose of your own path or others.

Alaric's human teacher was called Miss Czara, and the robot teacher was called Toyren. The classroom was a lovely light room, with various study areas. Each classroom had an outside space for private study and quiet time. All the children of all ages mixed on their lunch breaks to help with social interaction. The first school day started with introductions to remind the class of each other's names, then they had a meditation session. The day was then structured into various lessons that could alter depending on what the children needed.

It soon became clear Alaric had an aptitude for languages, maths and the sciences. There was also a small group in the class, including Alaric, who were displaying the telepathic abilities I mentioned earlier. The teacher put in place some study time to accommodate this so they could learn to harness this gift for the greater good.

This was quite an exciting year for Alaric as he also met his uncle Cael for the second time in his life. He could not remember the first time as he had been quite young, yet he was very familiar to him as he often saw him on the communication screen. Cael had taken a long overdue leave and was going to be on Earth for a couple of months, and as he had no home base there, he was staying with Alaric's family. This would be his home to travel from to see other people and places on the planet. Alaric was in awe of his uncle as he listened to story after story of his space adventures. He had spent time on a new moon station called Lunar, and then on Mars. Mars had two established human colonies that were stopovers for space travellers. He had also had the honour of meeting some Pleiadian high council members on their space station based near Jupiter. He also told him of some other ascension species he had seen, that humanity were slowly being introduced to; these were the Salcaritons and the Arcturians. The Salcaritons had the ability to be in any form that the individual species would understand, so they took on human form for Earth's understanding and comfort. The Arcturians are a very tall, graceful and slender race with a deep blue skin tone, and large elongated heads. He said they were a highly intelligent species yet somehow did not view themselves as superior. They are very supportive of Earth and are doing everything they can to support humanity's ascension. With the aid of Pleiadian technology, human space craft now had the ability to leave the solar system through the multidimensional travel portals.

The Pleiadians worked from one of their City ships, which was situated near the planet Jupiter and was docked at the Pleiadians space station that was based there. Cael told his family he had been assigned to a mission on a star ship that would leave the solar system from the Pleiadians space station. His experience of the last ten years in space travel had qualified him for this. His role was bridge officer, overseeing the navigation of the spaceship. He was very excited, but it did mean he would be away from Earth now for longer periods of time. At the age of thirty-two, he had not yet found his life partner as his career had always come first. But I know that you can have a life bond with a star ship crew member and be very happy, Baltrexn and I are the living proof. But our species could link mind-to-mind over great distances, which helps us easily adapt to isolation from each other.

For the two months Alaric's uncle was there he was his shadow, always asking for a story of his travels. I have to admit Cael did embellish them a bit for effect, but they were fuelling

Alaric's imagination, as he was also destined for this space life.

Life Journal – transmission 33
New Earth - The light beyond the horizon

The Earth years were rolling by, farm life had not changed much in Provence and Alaric's family was in good health. His grandmother was a bit slower, but her own health remedies and healing helped with this and I felt she looked a lot younger than her sixty-seven years. Vanina had grown into a very pretty ten-year-old. She had also inherited her father's height gene and had long, curly auburn hair now which was often plaited to keep it off her face. She was a very feminine girl, loved flowery dresses and was drawn to anything pretty. She could sew, did wonderful illustrations for her age, and loved the healing work she did with her mother and grandmother. Vanina was at school as well but had already decided at the age of twelve she would leave to train with her grandmother and mother to become a healer.

Alaric was also tall; he was well above his mother's height now, was very slim and he ate and ate, and his mother always used the Earth phrase 'you have hollow legs'. He had just turned twelve and had blossomed into a lovely, considerate young boy. He was top of his school in science and maths and his understanding of languages was way beyond what his teachers could instruct him in anymore. He was also developing his telepathic skills and again he needed to find a teacher that could enhance this ability further. His family were so proud of him, but I could see they were torn with these feelings as he was going to the space academy in the United States of America. His uncle had attended the same academy and it was the best in the world. Alaric had had an online interview and was accepted the next day. He was thrilled, so excited that I realised it had not yet dawned on him he would be away for long periods of time from his home, family and friends. Cael had taken some leave to come back to Earth and escort him there and see him settle in. This was a big relief to Jonas and Yulia, and they knew he would be in safe hands. Cael did feel a bit responsible for Alaric's decision to follow in his uncle's footsteps as he had encouraged him for years.

Prior to this life event, Alaric was joined by two new guides, Cashnon from the Pleiadians and Picicso from the Salcaritons. I had gone to the mission centre to meet them and we all brought them up to date on Alaric's life so far. Cashnon's purpose was to bring life balance to Alaric and clarity of mind, as over the next few years he was going to experience many new off-Earth world experiences. Picicso's role was to do with relationships and Alaric's interaction with others. Alaric was very bright with a very high IQ and often in humans we see this can isolate them from others in their relationship behaviour. For Alaric's life path it was key this was not allowed to happen.

The day quickly arrived for Alaric to leave his home and start the next phase of his life. He had gone around the whole farm the day before saying goodbye to the humans and robotic helpers and the animals. His parents had also laid on a party for him where everyone he knew was invited. There were many gifts and wise words given to him, and it was at this party that Alaric finally realised what this all meant. He was going miles away from all he had known for twelve years. I could feel his inner emotion, he felt upset inside but did not wish to show it as he knew one day, he would leave Earth and live on a space ship. He would always have a home to return to, as his uncle had.

He was travelling to the space academy in a gravity flying vehicle, and the journey would take about a one and a half hours. Cael reminded his tearful mother he would be only over an hour away as they boarded the craft. Alaric waved and as he turned away, he had a big smile on his face as his life was just about to change forever and he was going to live his dream.

Life Journal – transmission 34
New Earth - The light beyond the horizon

Alaric arrived at the space academy in just under one and a half hours of Earth time, but there was a five-hour time difference between his new location and his home. As the flying craft descended, he saw laid out in front of him a massive complex of what appeared to be glass buildings, strangely shaped structures and domes. As the flying craft left, he and Cael made their way to a large sweep of steps that led up to the front of the main building. He could see nearby landing pads with various styles of flying machines, some he recognised as space transporters. The whole area was landscaped with trees, fountains and flowing water grills with areas to sit. There were many walkways with floating signs pointing off to various destinations on the site. He saw small communal hover vehicles parked up that could take you wherever you wanted to go. Cael said they can be called to pick you up and they drive themselves, amazing technology that Alaric had not physically seen before – although he was well educated on all of these vehicles as it was one of his passions.

As he entered the building, he saw a hive of activity of humans, with lifts, moving platforms and stairs taking everyone to the area they needed to be in. A robot came up to them, introducing himself as Kelm; it already knew Alaric's name and destination. Kelm acknowledged Cael but his focus was on Alaric as he explained he was his assigned robot for his stay at the academy. Kelm took his luggage and placed it on a moving floating platform and reassured him he would be reunited with it later in the day. He took him and his uncle to where the new cadet recruits were meeting and after a few minutes they arrived at a building shaped like an upside-down boat with sails. There were many others gathering with them in this auditorium. His uncle explained this was the induction, and then they would be split into groups and have a tour of the academy. After that there would be a lunch where Alaric would meet up with him again. Kelm said he looked forward to seeing him later at his living quarters and quietly moved away, back the way they had come. His uncle had a meeting about a new mission, and he took off in a different direction, leaving Alaric standing there feeling a little bit bewildered.

Alaric was not alone for long though, as another robot came up to him and led him to his seat. He was sitting on the end of a full row of eleven children his own age. He looked around with wide eyes as he saw non-human forms; he knew they were Pleiadians and there was a Pleiadian youngling in his row of twelve. He found himself staring at her, she looked up and smiled at him and when he noticed her amazing eyes, they reminded him of sparkling blue crystals. I noticed his heart was beating faster than normal and his hands were sweaty and knew this was his first attraction to the opposite sex and he was confused. He had not seen a Pleiadian in the flesh, just on the global communication networks. All these feelings of excitement of being at the academy and now this, were a bit unsettling for him. But there was no time to dwell on it further as a voice boomed around the auditorium.

The induction lasted about an hour and was led by the famous admiral himself, Micaiah Delson. He was a tall, handsome, silver haired man with piercing blue eyes that were enhanced by his dark skin, and a commanding presence. He headed up the academy, but he was famous for leading and building the space program with the Pleiadians. Alaric had read all about him; this man before him had been to the Pleiadian home planets and seen many things Alaric could only dream of at the moment. When the induction was complete, a robot came to the end of their row and asked all twelve to follow him. Once outside the auditorium he explained he was their guide and his name was Frem.

Frem led them away to a recreational area, where they all sat in a circle with refreshments and introduced themselves. The Pleiadian he had been staring at was called Eyra, she spoke in a smooth musical voice that was captivating to Alaric. They were then led to the areas they would have their lessons in, and he saw the science rooms, the gravity chambers, meditation areas, language suite, telepathic and telekinesis rooms. Frem explained each section to them and answered any questions they had. He explained that as their time at the academy grew, they would eventually see the rest of the large site. They were then led to where the rest of the new cadets were all meeting up for lunch. Alaric's group was joined by the escorts who had brought them to the academy. His uncle Cael asked them all how they had enjoyed the morning, and savoured these young people's chatter and the visible excitement in their eyes. He was looking at a room full of the next generation of space cadets and was just as excited for them.

Eyra was joined at the lunch table by her mother, Cyvea. It turned out she was a member of the academy's council and a liason officer in the Earth's space program. They lived on the academy campus and she was thrilled Eyra was joining the cadet program. After lunch it was time for Alaric to say goodbye to his uncle, who was now heading back to his ship for his next mission. He told Alaric he would keep in touch with him through space transmissions, and to contact him if he had any questions or concerns. Alaric took a deep breath as his uncle turned and walked away, then he felt a hand on his arm, and saw that Eyra was by his side, smiling at him. She could feel his emotions and wanted to give him reassurance.

After lunch, Frem led them to their living quarters, explaining that this would be their home for the next four years of the cadet program. They were huge round domes and all the resting spaces looked out on a central covered courtyard. They all had their own room with washing and kitchen areas, and the courtyard was their recreational space. Their evening meals would be taken in the dining space they had their lunch in. Breakfast would be in their dome and lunch would depend on the lessons and activities they were doing. They were all assigned their own robot, which would see to their daily needs, cleansing of garments and rooms and their nourishment. Each dome had a room space for the robots to dwell in when not helping their assigned human. They also would run errands on the campus if needed, so they had a busy existence.

When Alaric entered his allocated room Kelm was waiting for him. Kelm had unpacked all his clothes and personal belongings but explained to Alaric he was to move anything he wished so he was comfortable. Somehow Kelm had everything put away in a sensible order, while the items on open shelves were easily accessible. He also saw his cadet uniforms hanging up, and wondered how they knew his size, and would they fit. Kelm had scanned him on arrival and picked the sizes needed so they would fit him perfectly. In one corner was the latest computer technology and Kelm showed him how it worked. This was not a computer like his at home; he now had a desk with a flat touch screen pad built into it. Kelm pressed an area of the touch screen panel, activating a screen that appeared in thin air, a touch frequency light energy screen. The robot explained he could control it with voice, mind thought and finger touch as well. It was linked to the global internet and the universal knowledge library. Kelm explained he would have restricted access on the universal knowledge library and he only had access to what would help with the academy teachings.

After the evening meal Alaric admitted he was tired, said good night to everyone and retired to his room. He laid on his bed remembering his day and a thought to contact home popped into his head. The next thing he knew, Kelm was awakening him with 'Rise and Shine,' and it was the next morning. Luckily, his uncle Cael had contacted his parents to say he had been safely delivered to the academy.

Life Journal – transmission 35
New Earth - The light beyond the horizon

My life on Diacurat has basically stayed the same as I transmit some of Alaric's life moments. Baltrexn's ship is still on its mission and I did get a timed long delayed short message from him saying he was well. I have sent a reply, but I am not sure when he will receive it. I am also pleased to say my historian online book is now approved and uploaded to the study library for the students to learn from. I have been asked to go and give a talk on my book to the students, so I am preparing for this at the moment. Every light day I cannot wait to look into my reflective self and see what has happened in Alaric's life.

After Alaric's induction day at the academy he settled into life there quite quickly. He got to know his fellow dome cadets gradually over a few weeks. He had become quite friendly with two young boys from his dome called Cashel and Solan. Cashel was from a region of Earth called Norway and Solan was from a region once called Russia. Russia was once a large country that had broken up into smaller regions of independence a hundred years ago and his home was in Valdaysky. Language was no barrier as they all spoke the unified global language, which is named English. They all were friends with Eyra, and the four of them could quite often be seen together out of class enjoying each other's company. I realised that this was a lifelong bond forming with these young beings. Alaric did get on politely with everyone and he often placed an energy distance barrier between himself and them. As we said earlier, he was so intelligent he did not always tolerate those who were not on his level and he could seem a bit detached at times. But for a life of meeting humans and ascension beings lying ahead of him, he needed to conquer this. His guide Picicso had been helping him work with relationships and trying to send likeminded people to him to build relationships with him. Cashel and Solan were on his level of understanding so he could have quite intense debates and conversations at higher-level understanding. We all saw Alaric needed to accept people of all intelligence levels and species so he could thrive in the space program.

The cadet program does teach this, but it is up to the individual student to accept these teachings in order to advance. Picicso advised us Alaric would have opportunities to meet all sorts of beings over the next four years and we would both encourage his mind to take them. To Alaric this would feel like an inner voice that humans call intuition, which encourages them on their rightful life path. A long time ago, the overseers created this process, which can be channelled through the soul by guides to the human heart centre and mind. They gave it the Earth word 'intuition' for light workers on Earth's level of understanding. As the higher self, I can also influence Alaric's decisions, but I will only be doing that if I am asked for help from the team of guides. My chief role is as an observer learning from this process.

Alaric's main lessons for his first year were mainly sciences and languages and he also had telepathic tuition. In the sciences, he was learning the science of multidimensional understanding, light and harmonic sound frequencies, and the science of gravity technology. He had been advised to study the Pleiadian and Arcturian languages, as he would come across these species in his cadet life and after. There were now language translators available on the star ships and he would also study how to use these; again, this was technology that had come from the Pleiadians. Eyra was helping him with the Pleiadian language, she had explained they live across three planets on their solar system and the basic dialogue can vary.

Alaric was also very interested in telekinesis – the moving of objects – and influencing their structure to manipulate them. He had asked to be considered for this, but the teachers wanted him to refine his telepathic skills more which would help build the capacity of his conscious mind. Eyra was a natural at telekinesis, as her species had mastered it centuries ago. She explained how they could manifest things and gave an example of how a doorway could be created in a wall by focusing on the energy frequencies of the wall materials. This was all done with mind control; once a species masters this manifestation technique, they can then take this to the next stage. This is the multidimensional body split where through mind control, they manipulate the body's base cell and molecules to transform into an ethereal form. They can then transform themselves back to physical form. I have explained this earlier in my incarnation process for you.

Alaric was a very keen student and progressed quickly with his studies. His next two years of life were focused at the academy on the campus, and visits home. The teachers wanted the basic knowledge and understanding of space to be taught before they could experience space travel in any form. Alaric found this frustrating at times, as Eyra often travelled back to her Pleiadian home world to see her father and family, and he longed to experience this. Her father had stayed on his home world to fulfil his role there. He was a leading scientist and oversaw much of what was happening on his planet. Her parents were not bonded and had decided Eyra should stay with her mother because of her interest in the Earth space programme. They also thought that in the future, Eyra would be a key member of this, as an ambassador liaising between their kind and humans. The one thing I had learnt working alongside Freylen is that Pleiadians always exist for the best of all not self, and all their decisions are made on this ethos of existence.

Alaric's parents had found time to be away from the home farm to visit him at the academy. I remember the first visit well as they were so in awe of the place. Alaric proudly showed them around and showed them his studies and what he had achieved. This first visit helped his parents understand his passion for becoming a space cadet and visualise his new way of life better. The bond with Eyra and Alaric had continued to grow as they spent a lot of time together out of lessons. She helped him with his telepathic skills and language skills. He had learnt so much about her way of life and the compassionate nature of her race. She never saw anything bad in anything. In her mindset, there was always a positive way forward and she never dwelled on past events.

Alaric's advancement in his telepathic skills had surprised his teachers, as he was progressing faster than his fellow students. A lot of this was down to Eyra's commitment to Alaric and his enthusiasm. She was teaching him the various facets to mind reading – for example, how to block others from reading your mind, and how to control your own power when you read another being's mind. He was learning to connect to Eyra's mind which obviously was not of human origin. Her mind already had the vast conscious sub core needed for this ability. The Pleiadians were born with their minds wired for this ability, and some lessons of guidance as younglings were all that were needed to guide and activate what was for them a natural process.

Alaric also loved watching Eyra use her telekinesis skills. This was a different process to telepathic skills; it was still mind control, but it was influencing matter. For the Earth understanding, materials are made from atoms made up of protons and neutrons which are held together by gluons. Human understanding was based on these named particles of existence. Every molecule, cell and atom and all that is within them has a frequency of unique vibrational existence that can be tuned into. The universe exists with light and harmonic sound frequencies that are part of everything with no exceptions. This is what the advanced intelligence of advanced minds can tune into. The human mind has to reset its thought processes for this activity; it's like a mental box that can be opened and shut just for this purpose. As with all mind control it has to be done safely without harm to others, in the harmony of love, not anger.

I recall the Earth day Alaric moved a drinking cup object; he was so surprised as he had been practicing for a long time with no results. He had got frustrated with himself and Eyra had explained this would prevent him from achieving telekinesis. He had learnt at last to calm his mind and find that box in the brain waiting to be opened. After that first breakthrough he learnt to levitate the glass in the air to his friend's amazement. This was great entertainment for them to witness. Eyra warned him to be careful when he did this as she had helped him, not his teachers. She advised him to speak to the teacher that headed up that telekinesis department and show him his newfound skills.

Life Journal – transmission 36
New Earth - The light beyond the horizon

Alaric's last two years of his academy life was even more exciting for him than the first two. He was now a handsome, tall, gangly young man aged fifteen. His body was rapidly altering towards human manhood and with this came new sexual urges. This was obviously a new experience for me, these human bodily urges that needed satisfying. One thing humans had learnt in their development and ascension over the last couple of centuries was to mentally suppress these urges, so they were only required for true love bonding and reproducing their young. He had felt these sensations towards Eyra and had struggled to act normally when near her, as he felt physically attracted to her at times. He had wondered if they were DNA compatible; he knew her reproductive organs were similar to an Earth female's, and Pleiadians bonded more through connecting mind and body energy rather than just physical release. Like many species, they often had no more than one or two younglings, and this would be pre-planned as it is on Earth. Alaric managed to work through his newfound sexual urges with his mind control over his physical body. His guides also helped to assist with this. This did not mean he did not want to be with Eyra, but he was sensible enough to know they were too young, and he should take this energy and focus it on his cadet career. He had not spoken to her about it as he was not one hundred percent sure how she felt about him. There were times when they were on their own, their eyes would catch each other's attention, and somehow the moment just stood still. They would both then quickly turn away and look for a new subject to talk about. It made me smile to witness this young love innocence.

One of the highlights in his third year at the academy was his first space trip to the moon colony. I recall his excitement as he helped Kelm pack for his trip. With his group of twelve students they travelled in a transport ship carrier to the space station above the moon. Alaric was attuned to how different this felt to the gravity Earth ships he had travelled on. The ships designed to leave Earth's orbit had to create the gravity field to sustain the human form in high speed space travel without disturbing their molecular structure. When humans have mastered the multidimensional energy, explained a few times in these transmissions, their space craft technology will alter to accommodate this.

Within the moon space station there was a mix of living quarters and docking stations for both Earth and off-world space ships. Apart from Eyra the whole cadet group was in awe of what they were experiencing, as this was the first step of their space journey through life. They were not on the moon space station for long as their shuttle to the moon ground station was ready.

When they landed, they docked with an airlock and their teacher led them through some tunnels to the main living area of the station. This station was called Moonwalker One and was part of a complex of stations that created the Lunar moon colony. The group quickly settled into their allocated rooms, which would be home for the next few days.

This was an educational trip where they were going to look at the history of the moon colony first-hand, and how the Pleiadians had assisted Earth's technology to help create this ground space station. As well as living areas, eating areas and science labs, there were large greenhouse structures full of plant life, with some also holding Earth's small animal species. Some of these were dedicated to supplying food substances for the colony members, supplementing other supplies being shuttled from Earth.

The Moonwalker One station also had a history display area of the moon, chronicling what humanity had discovered about the planet. Any ancient evidence from previous explorers of Earth who had landed there, had long turned to dust. They could only really discuss the geological composition and atmosphere of the moon, and how humans had conquered the challenges of living on it safely over the last century of Earth's time. To be honest, the whole purpose of the trip was to give the cadets their first experience of space and help them understand how humanity had reached this point in their history.

The next highlight of Alaric's year three was an expedition to Mars. This was a more extended trip, for a month of Earth time. Mars had been a dream living destination for humans for a long time, and in the twentieth and twenty-first centuries, they even made entertainment films of aliens invading Earth from Mars, and humans living on the planet, as their imaginations tried to understand this barren red planet in their skies. As I said in a previous transmission, this had once been a blue planet, similar to Earth, but not the same organically. An ancient off world civilisation had once made its home there and was destroyed when the planet atmosphere failed over four billion Earth years ago. This knowledge was uncovered as humans had found evidence deep within Mars' crust by using deep sonar scanning technology. There was some evidence of structures shaped like pyramids and cities. The overseers had no record of who they were, probably long since perished from the universe. With this advanced technology, they also scanned the surface to see where old oceans and land masses would have been. From this, they had created images and dimensional models of how Mars would have been over four billion years ago. Alaric found this all very fascinating as I did, with my history background.

I could see these amazing events really enhanced the cadets' thirst for more knowledge and experiences in space. The next huge event for them was in the second half of their fourth year when they were assigned to a star ship for one month in junior cadet positions. They would be allocated to an officer whom they would shadow. It would be an officer trained in the field the cadet wanted to specialise in.

Alaric spent time on his designated star ship with each working department. Because of this experience, he had decided he wanted to be a communication officer on a long distance star ship. By long distance I mean that he would be assigned to star ships that left his solar system to explore space within the intergalactic parameters. He had a natural mind for languages and had mastered the Pleiadian and Arcturian basic core languages very well. He also had a great telepathic ability and skill for reading beings' energy body language and ethereal fields, that all linked up with the communication process. There are language translators on the star ships, but when greeting new species in the future, it is good to greet them in their own language. Also, if they come across a new language in their space explorations, the communication officer studies this language and programs it into the translator for other species so they can understand it in their own language.

Eyra was also interested in languages but more from the perspective of a liaison officer, leading the contact to new species and planets that Earth humans made contact with. She also wanted to be part of this exciting new frontier of Earth's space exploration.

Life Journal – transmission 37
New Earth - The light beyond the horizon

The next event of celebration in Alaric's life was his graduation from the space cadet academy. He was now sixteen and a half Earth years old and a very tall, handsome young man. He looked very smart in his gold and blue parade cadet uniform, it enhanced his blue eyes and jet-black hair.

All his family were there, and I could feel their pride as it was reflected in their eyes. Vanina was wide-eyed at all these young handsome cadets. She was now fourteen years old, a tall, slender girl and a real beauty as humans understood it. Alaric introduced her to Cashel and Solan and to my surprise, while Vanina stayed cool and confident, it was Cashel and Solan who looked a little bit flustered. They laughed with Alaric later on about how he had kept his beautiful sister a secret. Alaric's uncle was also there, looking handsome in his full space uniform worn for ceremonies like this. His grandmother Aceso was there too, which was to Alaric's delight as she did not leave her home very often; she knew the importance of this day for the family and Alaric.

The graduation took place in the large parade ground that had tiered seating all around it, and in front of the raised platform at the front. They all took their places waiting for the ceremony to begin, a sea of faces as the whole academy was there with relatives and friends. There were floating air screens to help those who did not have a clear view, so everyone could see the cadets get their completion stars. The graduation cadets' families were at the front, so they had a clear view of the ceremony, which was led by Admiral Micaiah Delson.

I could really feel Alaric's excitement and nerves at the same time. The whole experience was quite enlightening, experiencing the energy and joy from so many beings. The moment came for Alaric to step up to the platform and he proudly strode towards the Admiral. They saluted each other and the Admiral placed the cadet star on his chest. The Admiral said congratulations, they saluted again, and Alaric turned to leave the platform to the cheers of his year group and his family. As the end of the ceremony drew near the Admiral talked about the highest award a cadet could receive from the academy, the Paragon Star. The admiral was saying, *"This award is for the student who has excelled and been a model of excellence, celebrating their skills, action and celebrity. They have been a role model for others to follow and a student who will be a future mentor to others."* The whole parade ground was silent. After a dramatic pause, Alaric heard his name announced as the winner of this prestigious award. He sat frozen as he heard an explosion of clapping and cheers from the whole parade ground. He felt himself standing up and moving forward, back towards the platform, having had no idea he was going to receive this prestigious award. He assumed it would be one of the others, as they had all worked so hard and excelled.

As he reached the Admiral and saluted again, they shook hands and the Admiral said how proud everyone was of him and his achievements at the academy. Alaric would set an example for the model student for years to come, and they looked forward to following his career in the Earth's global space program. They shook hands again and saluted and this time Alaric did not leave the platform but faced the audience, who cheered. He then led the way of tradition and took off his cap and threw it up in the air, and at this, the other graduating cadets followed with loud cheers. Alaric then jumped down to where the cadets were, they all surrounded him and lifted him up into the air, and the excited people in the parade ground cheered and clapped. The Admiral had a smile on his face, as the cadets carried Alaric off out the parade ground to carry on with the celebrations.

We were also very proud of my Earth friend and I know his guides had been working hard behind the scenes with his thoughts and energy. Alaric had been brought up in a very spiritual household with a great understanding of the soul and beings that guide humans. But he had never really connected to us, the reason being that he was the new generation of ascension humans who had adjusted his mindset to acceptance of all, including us. Alaric meditated daily, but for the purpose of clarity to enhance his telepathic mind and health. He was taking control of his mind and body in the fifth-dimension way of understanding. He and many others of this generation on Earth were laying the foundation for a human to exist in the fifth dimension energy without a high ascension soul.

The celebration of the cadet's graduation continued into late evening, with dining and dancing. Alaric's family had left earlier, all expressing how proud they were of him and promising they would see him soon. After the celebrations, the cadets would then have a couple of days to pack up their possessions and say their goodbyes before they travelled back to their homes. This time Alaric would travel back home alone; he was pleased to be going back, but could not wait to find out which star ship he would be assigned to. Eyra was staying with her mother, who still lived on the campus in her own dwelling, and this would be her home base when she returned to Earth after space missions. Her mother was very happy at the academy and was in a relationship with a human male called

Liton. He was the head of the telepathic and multidimensions section of the academy. He was an acclaimed man in his field with global expertise. They had started out as great friends and this had blossomed into a deep relationship and bonding. Eyra liked him and was happy for her mother, who seemed very happy.

Alaric and Eyra spent some time alone enjoying each other's company, neither wanting the moment to come they had to part. They knew they could communicate every day, but they did not know what their future held in their space careers and when they would meet again.

Kelm took Alaric to the travel craft allocated to take him home. The robot wished him well, there was no emotion from the robot as it was always very matter of fact and worked on the principles of truth and logic. But I felt Alaric would miss this machine and his robotic ways; he had after all been a part of his life every day for four years. Alaric took a deep breath as he entered the craft and did not look back.

Alaric arrived to a flurry of excitement at his homecoming. His old room had been freshly decorated and to his surprise there was a new computer like he had at the academy. His father Jonas said it was gift to him to reflect his achievements. Alaric took time to wander around the farm and enjoy this space again, reflecting on where his future would take him.

Life Journal – transmission 38
New Earth - The light beyond the horizon

Alaric spent two months at his home farm before his commission arrived. He saw the message from the global Earth space program and hesitated before he opened it. He had been in contact with his friends but none of them had heard anything yet. We were not surprised as we knew they liked the cadets to have some Earth normality before they were sent off on their future commissions.

He took a deep breath in and opened the transmission – it was from Admiral Belton, who led the space program. He welcomed him to the program and laid out his first commission and the ship he would be assigned to. He was going to the star ship Illustriouse and would serve under Captain Secora. He knew the ship was a model class one thousand with the latest technology, and was a long-distance star ship. The next part of the message said he would be a trainee communications officer and was assigned to Lieutenant Malone, who would oversee his training. They wanted him to report to the global Earth space centre base in five Earth days. For your information, the global Earth space centre base is located in a land called China. He had just finished reading his message when a transmission from Eyra popped up and he immediately connected. She was very excited, and they were amazed to discover they were on the same star ship. Her commission was trainee liaison officer which also overlapped with the communications department on board. She was assigned to Doctor Kiska, who was also the ship's counsellor. They both finished the transmissions so they could tell their parents the good news – or in Eyra's case, telepathically connect with her mother.

Alaric's parents were thrilled for him and very proud of the commission he had been awarded. He spent the next few days deciding what to take with him. He packed his best casual clothes and one possession from his childhood, the star ship model gifted to him by his Uncle Cael. That had been the moment in his life that had sparked his imagination and interest in space travel. He just wanted this item with him to remind him of his Earth journey and what led him to space. He felt there could be times ahead when he might need this space craft toy to ground him, to help him reflect and make decisions. We found it interesting how he needed something to hold onto from his past and we knew he would miss his home. Alaric also knew he would be well supported in the space program, but there was still that young human element of doubt lingering there.

Five days after receiving the transmission from Admiral Belton, Eyra arrived in a travel craft to pick up Alaric. They had decided to travel together to their new space commission. She had already meet Alaric's parents at the academy and was made very welcome. It was just a quick visit and the pair were eager to leave to start their new adventure in life.

Everyone came to wave goodbye to Alaric and Eyra, the travel craft hovered for a few seconds then speeded up and quickly vanished into the distance. It was about one Earth hour and 20 minutes to the global Earth space centre. They had seen images of the magnificent buildings that made up this base, created to reach the stars. Above it was a floating station the size of a large city. This sky city could move in the Earth's atmosphere to different locations if needed, but it mainly served the global Earth space centre base. The gravity technology had advanced to allow them to create this wonderful structure. As they approached the global Earth space centre base, they could see the city in the clouds was a hive of activity. Alaric wondered what all these humans did as small travel craft came and went, travelling off in all directions.

Their travel craft landed, and they were escorted to the main building terminal where they were met by communications officer Lieutenant Malone. He shook hands with Alaric and Eyra and explained he would escort them to the star ship Illustriouse. There was a robotic form with Malone that looked very human and they both could not help staring at this new advanced robot AI model. The robot was introduced as Tae and it served aboard the Illustriouse in a similar way Kelm did in the academy. But Tae was not assigned to just one human, it could be called upon by many, for various duties that needed to be carried out on board as well as on Earth. Tae left with all their luggage, taking it to the transporter ship they would travel in, to reach the Illustriouse star ship.

Malone explained that before they left, they were to be fitted out with their onboard uniforms and communication devices. They travelled through a high-speed tube system and stopped inside a domed building. They soon discovered this was where they were to be measured and fitted with everything they needed. Two robots appeared to escort them to the scanning area, where they were perfectly sized up for their uniforms, underclothes and shoes. Two hours later they both emerged in grey uniforms that were for the new trainees. Every rank had a different colour uniform, making it easy to identify each other on the star ship. Both sexes always wore trousers and tops as it was more practical in the work environment, the female tops were styled slightly differently, with a more feminine look to them. Malone's uniform was deep green, identifying his rank of lieutenant.

They made their way to the transporter ship and found themselves amongst a hive of activity. It was being loaded up with foods and technology as well as crew members. Tae joined them as they made their way to the refreshment rooms on board. Tae explained the food they saw would be stored in a form of cryoprotectant that preserved it until it was ready to be used. They also had a molecular cell processer that could create foods and drinks. This was state of the art technology Malone explained, and was being trialled on their ship. He also explained that the Pleiadian and Earth scientists were working together to create new technologies and told them about the new computer technology on board too. It was a piece of tech that would latch to the side of your temple without breaking the skin and then expand out into a clear, small screen over one eye. Its frequencies set to your brain waves and with mind thought control you could log into the ship's computer. Your brain saw a screen in front of you, in mid-air, which could be controlled in size, with your fingers or telepathically. Only you could see what was in front of you, and if others needed to share it, you could link to their screens. Alaric was wide-eyed at what he was being told, as he had not been aware of these new advancements. Malone explained they were trialling all this new technology to iron out any hiccups, then it would go worldwide, so they were seeing it first.

The transporter ship made its way to the Illustriouse, which was docked above Earth at the star ship station that built the ships. As it came into view, we felt Alaric's excitement and were so pleased he was going to be making this star ship his future home. The ship was long, and fifty stories high. The front of the ship was wider and rounder and this was where the main control bridge was. About two thirds of the way down, the ship had two large domes on each side which held plant life and recreational areas. Towards the end of the ship was the gravitational engines and the core, the multidimension section of the ship. Malone explained that when in flight, the core creates a shield of protection that surrounds the ship as they travel through space. The technology creates the gravity for survival within the ship, no matter what dimensional energies or gravity fields they encounter.

The moment came when they stepped on board this magnificent star ship and Malone led them to what would be their sleeping dwellings. They were on the same floor but a few resting spaces apart. They were comfortable spaces with a resting platform, comfy chairs, a working desk and cleansing space. Tae delivered their luggage and offered to help unpack but Alaric and Eyra politely declined, preferring to arrange their rooms as they wished. Malone explained there was a new trainee briefing at thirteen hundred hours and Tae would show them how to get there.

When the time came, they were led to a large room and there were twenty new trainees on board. Their individual mentors were also there, and Malone was busy introducing them all when the room fell silent and everyone turned to look at the door. Standing near the doorway was a tall, slim woman with slicked back blond hair who was silently surveying the room. All the mentors saluted and were then at ease as she walked towards them. Alaric had realised this was Captain Secora, as she stood there in a black and scarlet tailored uniform with her hands behind her back. She introduced herself and welcomed them all to the Illustriouse, explaining they would be answering to their mentors in their training days on board the ship. She then went to each trainee, individually welcoming them to the ship. Alaric felt a strong handshake and she congratulated him on receiving the Paragon Star.

I sit here with my mission team reflecting on Alaric's journey so far on Earth, and we all agree his life is on course for him to contribute to Earth's enlightenment journey. This will be through humanity making further contact with intergalactic members throughout the universe. The combination of this and humanity's progression on Earth will ensure their future amongst the stars.

Life Journal – transmission 39
New Earth - The light beyond the horizon

I met this light day with Havrium who oversees the incarnation program, as he wanted to see me to ensure I was fine with my journey so far. He asked me how I felt about Alaric and what sort of feelings I had experienced towards him. I understood this as meaning what attachments I had developed with him. I had actually been reflecting on this with Freylen the light day before and had asked about her experiences from her own Earth incarnation. She told me it was natural to have an emotional attachment to your Earth physical body link, as you live and feel their every thought and emotion. You naturally want the best for them, and it can be hard when this is not always achieved as you feel their pain and struggle. She also said you do have to learn to detach yourself from the emotional links and look at it logically as a learning path. She recalled when her reflection of self returned to her, she had a quiet time of healing and studying what she had learned from this experience with her mission team. She realised it had affected her own energy which was rebalanced during this healing time. The emotion was detached, and she was left with the memories of that Earth life experience, being able to logically look at it from all aspects of learning.

I explained to Havrium that this question had been on my mind, as I did feel protective of this human being. He explained it was natural to do so as you naturally want the best for him and humanity. Part of the learning is watching how humans learn from their own mistakes. He laughed and commented that if I had done an incarnation in around the years of the awakening over two hundred Earth years ago, it would have been a completely different experience for me. He said the mission team guides would have been working a lot harder and banging their heads against the walls in frustration. I laughed at this expression and he explained it was an old Earth phrase often used back in those times. Havrium finished the meeting, explaining he wanted me to try and prepare for the day the human I am attached to dies, as this is something all higher selves need to be aware of.

I knew in Alaric's case, like many of his generation, he had a human essence that was developing to a multidimensional ethereal soul level. This higher energy essence would be able to one day connect to the greater good light source energy of the universe. This connection would bring humanity into the fifth dimensional existence they are striving for. I felt honoured to have witnessed just a small fraction of what was occurring in this planet's continuing transformation.

On my return from meeting Havrium, I was also pleased there was a message from Baltrexn, letting me know they were estimating their mission would last for around one hundred of our light days. Freylen and I were now counting the light days until they returned to us.

I return to Alaric's Earth life three years on from the day he joined Illustriouse. He was now twenty years of age and a very confident, well thought of young man. He was near the end of his third year as a trainee communications officer under the watchful eye of Lieutenant Malone. They had become good friends over this time period, and he had given Alaric a lot of support in many ways.

Eyra had settled well into her role as communications liaison officer under the watchful eye of Doctor Kiska. Her role allowed her to be part of the ambassador's landing parties to planets they visited. Doctor Kiska was also used as an ambassador for building the links between Earth and intergalactic species they were introduced to. Illustriouse's role had developed into a star ship that carried ambassadors of Earth to various galaxies and solar systems to meet existing species, or ones that had been invited to join the Intergalactic Council. Alaric wanted to be a part of these parties as well, but he had to wait until he was qualified to the point that he had complete understanding of the communications processes and languages they knew of so far. His training program was usually five Earth years, but he had excelled in these three years. Unknown to him, Lieutenant Malone had agreed with Captain Secora that it was time to conclude his training. He felt Alaric would learn more now from new interactions with the species they encountered through landing missions. Malone was sure there was not much more he could teach him, and he suggested to the Captain that he would soon be learning from him! They agreed to promote him and send him on their next ground mission, with Lieutenant Malone attending in a support role.

In one of our mission catch-ups, we realised that this behaviour of Lieutenant Malone showed how humanity was now supporting each other. Yes, there was hierarchy and leadership, but humanity now had learned not to hold others back. They encouraged and helped each other even if this meant that person could excel quicker in their career than themselves.

We also discussed the continued growing relationship between Alaric and Eyra. So far it had been a platonic one, bound together with continued mutual support, common interests and spiritual understanding. Alaric had been knocked off balance lately as a new ship member had joined the crew, a Pleiadian called Kasmul. He had joined the engineering team and was a little bit older in Pleiadian understanding of Earth years. Eyra and Kasmul had been drawn together because they were the same species and had a lot to tell each other and catch up on about their own planets. This was the first time I had truly witnessed the jealousy gene in an adult human. Alaric kept all his feelings pent up inside, trying to understand this emotion he needed to let out. He started running the ship decks to release this inside turmoil he was trying to work through. Lieutenant Malone had noticed a difference in him as he seemed to be easily distracted, so on one of their joint runs he asked him what was troubling him. Alaric was hesitant at first, but he had to talk to someone, and he did not want it to be Doctor Kiska as she was close to Eyra and the ship's counsellor. Malone stopped running and took him to a quiet seating area. He quickly deduced this handsome young man in front of him was actually in love. He told Alaric he needed to declare himself to Eyra, or his feelings would start to affect his work and health. He realised he did have a lot to still teach this young man, but it was about human bonding relationships and how to communicate your feelings.

Malone had noticed Alaric was friendly with a few females and males but had not had a relationship with anyone. It was not discouraged on the star ship as they could be away from home for long periods of time. There were bonded humans with families on board and a small school and the balance of the community of the star ship was very important to the Captain and her crew.

Alaric spent a few days mulling over what Malone had advised, and finally plucked up the courage to talk to Eyra. He had invited her to the virtual entertainment suite, where he had booked one of the rooms. This was under the pretext of going on a bike ride through the Earth mountains of Spain to the coast. The technology of this Earth timeline was so advanced that it could create the sixth dimensional virtual reality with smells, breezes and noises. From what I could feel and see it felt very real. While taking their bike ride Alaric suggested they stopped on a view pint over the coastline. They settled down onto soft grass and relaxed. They were chatting and laughing like they always did when together, then Alaric took a deep breath and suddenly leaned forward, cupped Eyra's face in his hands and kissed her.

To Alaric it seemed the moment lasted forever with so many thoughts whirling around his head, the main one being, what if she rejected him? He pulled back and looked into Eyra's hypnotic blue eyes trying to read her mind, but he was too emotionally charged to see clearly. She placed a hand on the side of his head, pulling him back into a kiss embrace. It was a while before they came up for air and just lay there, watching the ocean in the distance. *"What's taken you so long?"* Eyra at last said to Alaric. He was not sure really, then scraped around his mind for the reason - it might have been the worry that they were not physically and mentally compatible. He had sometimes felt inferior to Eyra, because of her natural ascension abilities. Also, if they wanted to take it beyond just a physical relationship to a life bond of commitment, could they have children? Being in clarity of mind, Eyra could read his thoughts and said, "Don't worry what the future brings, we will take it a day at a time and see where our lives take us. Let's enjoy the moments we have together at a steady pace and our love for each other will unfold. We will have to accept whatever our journey is, as two different species joining in a relationship." She reminded him that her mother was in a relationship with an Earth man, and this had been accepted by both species. Compatibility of DNA was yet to be fully explored, but the Pleiadians were very advanced in genetics. For thousands of Earth years, they have assisted the Intergalactic Council with human DNA, and their own species' DNA has been used in humans.

After their declaration for each other they returned to their living quarters hand in hand. Many crew members who knew them well, nodded and smiled as they walked on by, many thinking, *about time too*.

Life Journal – transmission 40
New Earth - The light beyond the horizon

Lieutenant Malone spoke to Alaric about his training as a communication officer and congratulated him on how well he had done. He told him they had decided he had completed this in three years and would qualify as a junior ranked communication officer. He would be awarded the rank of Corporal first class. Alaric was not surprised it was concluding two years early, as he knew how well he had been doing. Also, his telepathic progression link which he had been practicing with Eyra had enhanced his sixth sense of knowing what people are thinking and feeling. This was an ability to sense their thoughts through their energy frequencies, without invading their mind space.

Malone explained to Alaric they wanted him to join them on their next planet ground mission, which was in a few days' time. He wanted Alaric to use his communication skills and sixth sense to read these beings they were visiting and their intentions to Earth and the Intergalactic Council. He also explained that after every mission they have a debriefing and he would be asked to be part of that process too. Alaric was thrilled – this was what he had been working towards and he could not wait for the ground mission to commence.

The mission was to a planet called Castrolian. It was a long journey for the Illustriouse, but they used space portals to jump the distance needed to get there. I was thrilled this was one of the planets they were visiting, as I had also been there in my role as a historian. I had gone with a science expedition to study this lovely healing planet and its history, and we had been made very welcome.

To describe where this planet is means taking you far, far away from the Earth's solar system, millions of light years as Earth humans call the distance in space. It is a planet that orbits a light star which is larger than Earth's; Castrolian is one of twelve main planets within their solar system orbiting around their light star. Castrolian is smaller than Earth and orbits a larger planet. I think this larger planet bears the closest resemblance to the planet Saturn's appearance in Earth's solar system, and a couple of moons also orbit this planet. Castrolian does have some similarities to Earth; it has a liquid substance that helps to sustain life, as water does on Earth, but the make-up of the liquid is chemically different and is a life source produced from inside the planet. The planet has plant life, animals and physical energy beings inhabiting it. Its history of existence is all very similar to Earth's timeline and solar system.

The landing party was made up of Captain Secora, Doctor Kiska, Kyra, Lieutenant Malone, Alaric and a couple of the science crew. The humans had to wear bio support life suits, as the atmosphere on Castrolian was not exactly the same chemical make up as Earth's. Eyra had the ability to adapt to different atmospheres as long as they were not too toxic, and she was fine on this planet. The reason for the arranged visit was the Castrolians had been asked to join the Intergalactic Council community. This was the first mission to confirm this and lay out the Intergalactic Council parameters and how they would both benefit from the alliance.

They met at Jestdol, their main city, and Alaric immediately sensed a peaceful people that were no threat. He had studied the information in the star ship's computer records of the planet before the landing mission. As to the rulers of Castrolian, they had overseers for each populated city areas;

there were six in total around the planet. For example, Jestdol had twelve elders who oversaw the community; they were elected for their experience to ensure their values were maintained, and especially that they were taught to the young and fully explained. Remember the access to the universe knowledge pot; this showed them new technologies and other places, but with their clarity of thinking, they know to take just what serves them all for the best – for example, their method of flight was an idea from this pot of knowledge. They also knew not to invite lesser ascended beings to visit their planet, or take on new technologies they don't understand or that would not serve the greater good, as this could destabilise their way of life. Now they had ascended to this early fifth dimension energy level, they were ready to join with the Intergalactic Council and explore beyond their world to serve the greater good.

The inhabitants of Castrolian were part of a civilisation of beings who are very ethereal in nature. They protect their planet and live in a spiritual existence with each other. They have ascended to a point where there is no hate or anger amongst them, but like humans, they do have a lot of emotions – for example, they suffer pain and loss when one of their own dies or is physically hurt. Alaric realised they were in a similar position to Earth; they had ascended beyond the fourth dimension and were now ascending into the fifth-dimension way of thinking and being.

They had developed telepathic powers and spoken language for communication, with the dialects varying slightly around the planet. They had now progressed, and the spoken language was becoming less important as the telepathic mind expanded. With entering the fifth energy frequency, their consciousness is expanding to aid this telepathic progress. This was a peaceful world, and they had never segregated themselves, as Earth did once, into different races and religions. They lived in communities around their planet assisting and helping each other, and this has assured their survival. As you know, planet Earth has its hot and cold climates, but because of the way this planet was situated within its solar system, enjoying the protection of a larger planet, they did not experience the same extremes of climate. They had a seasonal existence and their days and nights were shorter than Earth's, but they did not live by time restricting their lives – they had ascended beyond that. There was a time when their civilisation was more focused on timekeeping, but they have now grown out of the third-dimension limited way of thinking and now they see everything differently.

As you can imagine, the ascension of this planet has been very interesting to the Intergalactic Council, as these beings never had the destructive tendencies humanity once had. They also had the soul connection as earthlings do, and they were ascending to a point where this would no longer be needed. I must add here I have been told that being a soul connection or guide linked with these beings is like a peaceful, restful holiday. This planet gave the overseers hope for all beings from what we have learned from this planet called Castrolian.

Alaric observed the males and females were similar in appearance, but the females were more delicate in features and slightly smaller than the males. They had pale lilac skins and fine silver blond hair. Just above their brow was a section of skin over their bone structure that protruded out and then receded, which is the start of their hairline. The hair was straight and usually long for both sexes. He had checked their physical makeup before leaving the ship, and found they had the equivalent of lungs and heart, while the liquid in their veins had a translucent glow to it. They had no kidneys or liver, but a food filtration system in their body that does all this for them. They had three very long, slim fingers and a thumb equivalent, and feet with four toes. They had no body hair apart from on their head, mainly due to the constant warm climate they had adapted to.

He thought when he first saw a group of them, they were all very similar in appearance. But as he adjusted to their world and got to know them, he could understand the differences, that they each had individual personalities and uniqueness about them. He was told they have a general life span of 90 to 150 years of Earth time, and the planet population is a lot smaller than Earth's. Most Castrolians mated for life and had no more than one or two children.

Their visit was to be over a few days, going back and forth to the planet as needed. As part of their visit they were invited to a matching ceremony. The elders wanted them to witness part of their traditions while they were there. Castrolians are drawn to their partners by an inner connection, quite often bonding when young, and hold a matching ceremony with their whole community present when the time is right for them to live and bond together. At the ceremonies they played music through long crystal pipes that they danced to, while an elder of priest status oversaw the ceremony. They wore their ceremonial clothes decorated with gems and crystals, which are easily found on the planet's surface, especially near the flowing energy sources. On this special occasion, they used their world's flora to decorate their hair and ceremony area, appreciating the beauty of their nature, and believe me, it was beautiful to hear and see.

Eyra was interested in the garments that covered up their form, which were mainly practical clothes and made from a plant that they processed and wove into fabric. The nearest texture to this on Earth would be your silk, but theirs has a tougher fibre. Alaric told her their lighting came from a crystal that absorbs the sun's energy and reflects out the light when it's dark. They also had another crystal stone that gave out heat absorbed from the planet's energies and light star, which was used for a mixture of warmth and cooking.

They also both observed their communication was through spoken language, telepathic means, technology and travel. Their telepathic skills were very enhanced, overriding the spoken language. Their main source of travel was flight, for which they used a clean, crystal-based energy source with rechargeable properties. Their flight machines did not have wings – they used a gravity technology power source that raised them from the ground and propelled them to their destination. They also had boat crafts as they enjoyed their equivalent of a water source on their planet, and these crafts hovered across the flat energy lakes as well as the flat parts of land. The machines were made from a single mineral metal source that could be manipulated to their needs. Extraction of this was closely monitored and came from one part of their planet.

They also had a chance to visit their personal homes, where they observed resting areas, mainly used to rest their minds; during sleep, the tentacles from their gills plugged into their planet's source of energy. This was a vine-like growth that came from a special plant; the vines appeared to have pulsating veins, which contained the energy from the planet source.

Development of the young Castrolian being was so different to Earth's. They were also fascinated by the pods their young developed in. They carried the seed of life within each gender, and when they met the mate of their choice, they chose the time to have their young. The female released an egg cocooned in a transparent hard shell, which came from an organ like a small gill on the side of her body; the male then released fertilisation pods from his gill that sprinkled over the shell of the egg. The shell was then safely placed in an environment incubator connected to the planet's life source. Tentacles formed from the shell to link to the planet source of life force energy and as it did, the outer shell turned a light purple. The young being was nourished by this planet energy source, helping the young Castrolian being to grow, developing its gender, individual essence and character while cocooned in its own shell.

The development period of the pod was equivalent to seven Earth months. The chemical change on the outside of the pod darkened to a deep purple, which was a sign that all was ready for the little being to come into the world. A natural crack appeared around the pod and fell away, and the new life emerged with its parents' assistance. The egg pods were placed in their homes for the development and growth period, connected to the plant life source. The pods were always watched over with excitement and love.

The planet was alive, full of energy and its history was recorded into deep-set crystal cores and the Castrolian teachings. Through time, the physical beings of the planet connected to this source for life and education. The knowledge held in the planet's crystal cores was transferred to the energy source for the Castrolians to absorb deep into their minds. This was a bit like transferring a planet's DNA pattern of thought, and they had also learnt to telepathically transfer knowledge and images into crystals themselves. They used shafts of crystal about eighteen inches long and one inch across, which were hexagonal and placed into their technology. The technology could then reflect this information in imagery around the Castrolian using it, or connect to their thought patterns. Due to their ascension level, they can also now take themselves into the situation or the subject and experience it as if they are part of it. This is a bit like the virtual reality experience Alaric and Eyra had when they enjoyed the virtual bike ride in Spain.

The landing party also observed the planet's nature and animal kingdom while on the planet. The most similar animals to Earth were horses, but they were taller with longer necks, running in herds and very spiritual. There were various other creatures very much like those on Earth, such as the cat family, as well as flying creatures that lived off the nectar of plants, and creatures that burrowed in the ground. There were also predators amongst Castrolians creatures that lived off each other as well as off vegetation and the planet energy source. There was a natural order to things in their animal kingdom, which if uninterrupted helped keep the creatures' populations under control. Their habitats remained untouched and the planet's nature was allowed to stay balanced as the Castrolians respected her and understood that for their survival, it was important the planet was unpolluted. The animals lived in harmony with the Castrolians and connected to the planet source of energy; through their evolution, all of these beautiful beings understood this.

The debriefing after the visit was positive. Alaric and Eyra contributed greatly to the meeting with very insightful assessments of this beautiful race and planet. Their mentors were delighted with them both. They were all very pleased a foundation had now been laid with the Castrolians for their future in the Intergalactic Council. The Illustriouse and other star ships would return to them many times in the future to continue to build on this foundation. Eyra also received a promotion elevating her to Liaison group counsellor.

Life Journal – transmission 41
New Earth - The light beyond the horizon

The star ship Illustriouse was the original long-distance flag ship for the space program and led the way for more star ships, with each one's technology more advanced than the last. Alaric kept up to date with the newer models and what they offered, especially in the communication field. He felt they had become too robotic and it was important when meeting new civilisations on new planets that they meet the human not the technology they had created. He had made the decision to stay on star ship Illustriouse after being offered a position on another ship. It was a wise move because at the age of twenty-five he took over from the newly promoted Major Malone's position as Major class one head of communications. Major Malone took up a position as a second officer on a new star ship, which was a great promotion for him. Alaric now had his own cadets to train and was part of all landing parties when the star ship's ambassadors met new species.

He loved his job and we were very proud of how far he had come, just as his Earth family was. He rarely visited Earth now, but had regular updates with his family. He and Eyra had returned the previous year for his sister's wedding. She had married a local man who was a craftsman and they both lived on the family farm, helping his grandmother and parents.

The relationship of Eyra and Alaric had blossomed, and they now shared a larger resting space together. They had bonded in their physical relationship and their commitment to each other. Neither thought of marrying; it was not really expected of young couples in this new age. They were so compatible and living and working together only brought them closer. They had taken some time to look into having a child together and had discovered some other humans and Pleiadians who had conceived a hybrid child. But this was achieved by some genetic adjustment of the fertilised egg before it was placed in the Mother host. They had thought they would wait a bit longer as both were so busy with their lives and work. But then they decided they might never be ready, so they decided to go ahead and let life take its course.

I have just met with the mission team again and they felt Alaric had really been living his life mission. He had contributed so much to the space program in his own way, helping to bring Earth more into the fifth dimensional framework of the universe. All the worry of whether or not he could accept others and relate to them had been unfounded. The guide team realised they had conquered this by bringing in the human support network of other humans on his lifeline, like Lieutenant Malone. His relationship with Eyra was also key, as she had a huge compassionate heart as well as being able to read people and any situation for what it was. She had guided Alaric from the day they had met, but in a way, he did not always realise she had.

Alaric was in his twenty sixth year when his daughter was born. She was a delicately framed, small baby like her mother, her skin tone and hair were more human. She had a tuft of light strawberry blond hair and her mother's eyes. They both sat there in wonder at this tiny being they had created and wondered what life would have in store for her. I was surprised at the instant rush of love that Alaric felt for this child, it seemed stronger than the love he had for Eyra. Freylen explained that it's a different love you experience for a child on Earth, an overwhelming feeling of protection, and you would give your life for them without hesitation. I was yet to have a youngling but wondered if this would be the same for us.

Alaric and Eyra named their daughter Seren, meaning 'star' in the Earth language; it seemed to fit well as she was born on the star ship. It was lovely to see Seren growing up through Alaric's eyes as a father. When she was six months old, they took some leave and went to Earth for their families to meet her. Eyra's mother Cyvea and her partner Liton joined them for a few days. While they were there, Alaric's sister Vanina announced she was expecting their first child in seven Earth months. It was a wonderful few days with the family together, they all had a lot to be grateful for and celebrate together and of course, little Seren was the star of the show.

Seren's life on a star ship was a natural process for her as it was for many children in this new Earth age of being. She was loved and secure and everybody knew and adored her. By the age of two she was talking well and had a natural ability for telekinesis. They used to catch her giggling as she was juggling her toys with her mind. Her telepathic skills were also obvious; often before she was asked to do something she would go and do it or decide not to and hide. Her parents realised how unique she was, as well as very bright, which could be a challenge with a willful, strong-minded child.

I could see how much Alaric adored his little girl; she had changed his perspective in life. Everything he did now was for their future, securing a life they could all thrive in. They had actually talked of going back to Earth and joining the academy as teachers or advisers. This would give a more normal upbringing for Seren, but they would miss this way of life. Cyvea had put feelers out to the academy council and they said they would jump at the chance to have them both as teachers, mentors and advisers as they were such distinguished ambassadors for the space program.

By the time Seren was four, after many long discussions, Alaric and Eyra decided to leave their space life and return to Earth before Seren reached the Earth school age of six. The academy was delighted and started to make plans for their return, but processes had to be put in place on the star ship, one of these being to find their replacements. Captain Secora tried to persuade them to stay, as they were such a key part of their missions and had built up a superb reputation throughout the galactic members. But she also realised that any future space cadet under their wing at the academy would have an amazing experience due to their years of space travel and knowledge. While all of this was being sorted, star ship life and their missions continued as before.

Life Journal – transmission 42
New Earth - The light beyond the horizon

Their next mission was visiting the star system called Quipquim. Among the planets was one called Collpol, with a race of beings that had evolved over a million Earth years of time, into a very advanced society. They were very tall, slim beings of around eight foot in stature with a leathery skin of green tone. They were cast in the human form with a large upright, elongated head and had what you would understand as six fingers and toes. They had spoken language and were not telepathic but had intense sensory perception. Their planet had been through eternal wars that nearly destroyed them, but this was their wake-up call. They managed to salvage their planet and save their kind and evolve again into the peaceful society they are today. They had just one cloud hanging over them and this was a dark force of beings called Tablorns, who kept attacking their planet and star ships. They were from another star system and they had the technology to travel across space but due to their destructive behaviour they were not part of the Intergalactic Council. The Council had been aware of them for a long time and had managed to avoid them until now.

The Collpol had approached the Intergalactic Council to seek support and to help them stop these dark force beings harming them. Alaric discovered the planet Collpol contained a substance called Picrum, which the Tablorns wanted to use as a fuel base substance. Their own planet's resource was depleted, so they scoured the star systems to plunder it. Rather than asking and making trade deals they tried to dominate other species or raid the planets with use of force.

The Earth space program had equipped their star ships with a few weapons, but they were rarely used. They also had some star ships that were heavily armed and used as extra support and they flanked other star ships in rare cases like this. In the case of the Collpol, the Intergalactic Council had accepted the plea for help, as they were a society that fitted the criteria to join the Intergalactic Council. They had been aware of the Collpol and there were thousands of planets throughout the universe that the council had not yet approached.

The Collpol had tried to contact the Tablorn and negotiate with them, but they answered this with another raid that killed some of the people. Alaric had managed to translate some of their language to enable the Intergalactic Council to contact the Tablorn and draw up a peaceful trade deal. But unfortunately, they made it clear by attacking an Earth star ship that they were not willing to negotiate. They had also discovered they had attacked other planets with sources of Picrum, and many of these planets could not defend themselves as they did not have advanced technology weapons.

The Tablorn had caused quite destructive damage which was not needed. They were such an aggressive species from a dark negative force of nature that the Intergalactic Council decided the only way to resolve the crisis was to attack their scout ships. This was a very rare action for the Intergalactic Council to take as they were of the light and looking for peace not war, but they had no choice but to defend these peaceful worlds and themselves.

When these missions to find the Tablorn scout ships was completed, the Intergalactic Council felt it was safe again for the Collpol. They gave them knowledge of advanced weapon systems that could be placed above their planet for protection and deep space scanning technology. When this was in place, they would be able to protect themselves better and the hope was the Tablorn would leave them alone. The Intergalactic Council had made it clear to the Tablorn they were willing to negotiate and offer them knowledge of looking at their home planet for other ways they could create fuel. Once the Tablorn realised they were being prevented from seeking the substance they sought, and were out-maneuvered by brains and technology, they opened up to talks.

The star ship Illustriouse was given this mission of peace as its crew was the most experienced in the space program. There was a bit of apprehension amongst them, as this was different to all the other missions. This time they were dealing with a race who thought they were superior to all other species and were not used to negotiating. The mission party was made up of Captain Secora, Alaric, one of his colleagues and two counsellor ambassadors. There was also a small armed security team with this mission, due to the aggressive nature of this race. The team felt well prepared with the language translator Alaric, who had prepared thoroughly for this purpose.

The mission away team took a small space shuttle down to the meeting point on the Tablorn planet's surface. They landed on top of a large green building, in a very large and densely populated city where, in fact, all the buildings were green. They looked like solid blocks next to each other, but of different height and size, going off in all directions as far as the eye could see. The planet's atmosphere was very toxic to them, so they had their bio suits on. The suits were like normal clothes but had special technology to protect and monitor their vital signs. They wore sealed gloves and an unobtrusive helmet for air supply, provided by a small processing unit attached to their waist belts. There was no limit to their stay as the air processing unit was self-powering, taking the energy from the space around them. Alaric noticed the grey-purple cloudy sky; he could not see a light star and the atmosphere was very condensed, creating thick clouds. He thought it all looked quite gloomy and depressing.

They were met by a Tablorn welcoming committee that included rows of armed guards, and it was obvious they were trying to intimidate this peaceful mission convoy. Alaric was sure it was just show; the fact they were meeting with them was a great breakthrough, even though the Tablorns' hand had been forced.

They were taken through a tall ceilinged room to another room where they were invited to sit. Eventually, three very distinguished looking Tablorns came into the room, greeting the mission team enthusiastically and delighted that the team could reply in the Tablorn language. The team discussed the options of forming a peace treaty. Part of this deal was that they would help them source peacefully the Picrum, while looking at other possibilities to fuel their world. After what seemed a long period of ironing out any translation problems for clear understanding, they came to an agreement. Alaric had a big feeling of relief and could not wait to leave this place as it gave him a feeling of foreboding and danger.

They all stood up and moved to greet each other, sealing the new friendship with the agreed treaty, when there was a commotion at the entrance to the room. Six armed Tablorns ran forward, firing deadly pulse beams at the team and the three Tablorn officials who had just agreed to the treaty. One of them fell dead to the ground while the others all ran for cover while the mission's security team was firing back at the six Tablorns. In the chaos, no one had seen Alaric fall silently to the ground behind the seating area. Eventually, the six Tablorn were dead, killed by their own guards and the mission team's security team. Silence fell with disbelief from both sides at the two deaths.

Life Journal – transmission 43
New Earth - The light beyond the horizon

This had been the moment Havrium had told me to prepare for, the death of my chosen Earth body, Alaric. We knew when this was to happen and I was at the mission centre with all the incarnation mission team preparing for his death. I had linked with my reflection of self during this time frame. His death at the age of thirty-two Earth years had been instant, and I sensed he did not feel any pain. As his heart stopped beating, the reflection of self soul energy released with his human essence and memories. We all connected with the Earth reflection of self soul energy, guiding it back through the light harmonic sound technology transporter to the suspension energy chamber. I was asked to step into the monitoring pod that would observe my physical body functions. I felt my physical form being lifted and then I was suspended in mid-air, floating in a light harmonic energy field. I felt calm and my physical form slowed down into a stasis state of being. When this was established, they blended my reflection of self in the light harmonic sound particle transmitter with my ethereal and physical self. I was surrounded by a light harmonic sound beam that helped with the re-blending of my reflection of self to my physical form.

I could feel myself adjusting to this energy and my mind was absorbing Alaric's Earth life and all the memories, sensations and feelings the human body experienced. When complete I was released from the suspension energy chamber and felt as if I was running on a higher frequency, my mind trying to deal with this massive download. I was very tired and went to the rest chamber where I fell into a deep sleep. My mind and body needed to re-adjust itself, and my mind's deep consciousness needed to evaluate and deal with this Earth life and everything that came with it. All this information was downloaded into the memory bank of the universal knowledge library where all our meetings and assessments were held too.

I actually slept until the next light day and woke up very hungry. I had a large, nourishing breakfast, then the mission team asked to monitor me again just to check I had rebalanced with the absorption of reflection of self. When they were happy with me, I went back to my home dwelling to rest further. Havrium had arranged a mission team meeting the next day where we would start evaluating the reflection of self download and the lessons learnt. I would also receive any healing needed so my mind and body were fully adjusted after this Earth incarnation experience. I have to admit I was still feeling a bit detached from it all and Freylen said this is normal. I have to deal with any attachments I had to Alaric and analyse my role as an incarnated soul in an Earth body.

I was grateful for Freylen to talk to as a friend, as I could not communicate with Baltrexn yet. We went to the mission team meeting where we discussed Alaric's life. His mission was to bring himself to the forefront of the space program's innovation team, leading the way with connection to new worlds, and to bond with a new species and produce a hybrid child, who would become a key member of new Earth's future society. The unions between human and Pleiadians would start to change the human race makeup, aiding their ascension. We all felt this had been achieved and we evaluated the work of the guides. The consensus of opinion was they had been very successful and contributed to the New Earth's energy, building on the light energy around the planet.

As for me, I knew I would need to adjust to this experience as Alaric's life was now part of me for always. I can detach myself from the experience and call on the memories when I choose. Freylen said she often revisits her Earth life, but with no emotion, just a reminder of the experience and what she learnt from it. If I wish I can also look in on his Earth family, as their lives continue without him. I did look in on his life end dedication which was held in his hometown. All his friends, close crew members and family were there, many with disbelief that Alaric had been taken so young.

I also checked in on Eyra to see how she and Seren were coping after Alaric's death. Eyra had opted to stay on the ship the day of the mission as Seren had been a bit under the weather. Later they heard there had been an attack and two people were dead. Eyra knew one of them was Alaric as she could not feel his life force anymore. The crew found her in the corner of their living quarters, rocking to and fro, and holding on tightly to Seren. These emotions came from her core and were new to her. As you can imagine the ship's crew did everything to support them both, but Eyra just felt numb. She was living her life but could not feel anything and wondered if she ever would again. She knew Alaric would want her to be strong for Seren and bring her up the way they had planned.

After Alaric's life dedication service, Eyra went to live at the academy with her mother. She wanted the students to know of this amazing human being and what he had done for the alliance with the Pleiadians. She wanted her daughter to grow up being proud of her father and his achievements for humanity. Eyra became his voice, teaching her knowledge to whoever would listen. Alaric would have been so proud of

Eyra and what she was achieving in his name, as I was.

The last time I looked on how they were doing at the academy, they had erected a statue of Alaric as a tribute. This was a proud and very emotional time for his loved ones, and I thought what an honour it was for his memory. We had contributed to this unique human being and I was proud to have been part of his human Earth life.

Life Journal – transmission 44
New Earth - The light beyond the horizon

My time with Alaric would never be forgotten, but naturally my life was moving forward, and today was the light day Baltrexn and Siroian returned from their space mission. They had been away for one hundred light days and I had really missed him. I had had amazing support from my incarnation mission team but I had missed our mind links and his energy around me.

Freylen had come to my dwelling to wait with me and we were both very excited. Finally, the moment arrived and we both went outside to greet them as they arrived and to my delight, Siroian embraced Freylen and held her as tight as Baltrexn held me. We talked for a long time about all our adventures over a meal Freylen and I had prepared. As night descended Siroian and Freylen departed so we could all have our private energy exchanging moments together.

A few light days passed before we all met up again. Freylen and Siroian were very excited and announced they were going home to Pleiadian to bond for life. We were so excited for them both and we all embraced to savour the moment. They wanted to go home for the bonding ceremony so both their families and friends could celebrate with them. We were delighted to be invited and knew we had lifelong friends in this pair of beautiful beings. They would come back to Diacurat to live while Siroian was commissioned on Baltrexn's star ship.

We also shared our news that we were committed to having a youngling but asked them to keep it a secret until I had conceived. This was a huge decision for us both as we knew how much a youngling would change our lives. From my experience with Alaric, I had realised how younglings can change your focus on life. The only other being I had told was my mother, as I wanted her to enlighten me about what it was like to have a youngling. Of course, being my mother, she saw me as the light of her life; she reminded me you never stop wanting the best for your children, no matter their age. We had decided Baltrexn would carry on with his career and I would just slow mine down a bit. I was going to focus on teaching my history discoveries to young students keen to learn. I was going to do the talk about my history book in a few light days, so I felt very positive about the future.

Later, we both sat on our veranda looking out over the lake. It was so peaceful as we watched the light star fade over the horizon. I felt very lucky to have the fulfilling, unique life I had enjoyed so far. I was reflecting on my Earth incarnation experience and the history I had discovered about that ancient planet. It was wonderful to see how eventually, after thousands of years, the Earth human race had ascended into the fifth dimensional existence. This had allowed the ascension beings of light to embrace their planet and guide them forward on this 'New Earth'.

I look forward to the light day I hear Earth is no longer one of the planets used in the incarnation program. Humanity will then be existing in the fifth and sixth dimensional existence. They will be joining many ascended beings throughout the universe, engaged in the cause of bringing the light to beings existing in the darker energies. They might choose to do this by joining the incarnation program themselves or travelling on the many universal star ships, helping other ascension races spread the message of love and light.

... Transmission ends

About the Author

Sharon from Bengalrose Healing is a medium, author, holistic healer, spiritual teacher and mentor based in the United Kingdom. Her ninth book, 'New Earth - The light beyond the horizon', is part of a collection of books she has written. 'Utopia', 'The Magic of Spirit', 'The Magic of Words', 'Ayderline the Spirit Within', 'Step into the Mind of a Medium', 'Heavenly Guidance', 'The light within Atlantis', 'Your daily spiritual guidance diary' and 'Inspiration Guidance Cards'.

Sharon is also the founder of the 'One Spiritual Movement' community   www.onespiritualmovement.com
Facebook one spiritual movement

Sharon's books are available on Amazon and on her own website: www.bengalrose.co.uk.

Visit her website www.bengalrose.co.uk to find out more about Sharon and what she offers.

You can also find her on twitter @SBengalrose and FaceBook Bengalrosehealing.

Sharon has a YouTube channel with over one hundred fifty spiritual guidance videos. Search 'Sharon Bengalrose'.

Sharon also welcomes contact through
email: Sharon@bengalrose.co.uk

Printed in Great Britain
by Amazon

62110611R00139